BM

W9-BGN-900

# The Treasures We Leave Behind

Joy P. Gage

For Her. For God. For Real.

faithfulwoman.com

## Here's what people are saying about Joy Gage and *The Treasures We Leave Behind*

Joy Gage is a life-long friend, a sister and mentor.
Is sister too strong a word? Never.
Throughout our lives we were Christian siblings in search of God's
   will—
I should have known—she has a trunk too!
Hers has the same kind of stuff mine has in it—
The relics of our life Exodus.
Our trunks are the arks of our covenants with God—
They contain the holy relics of our pilgrimage.
Things we picked up in flight from Egypt.
Things so precious we dare not leave them behind—
The manna that fed us when we hungered after God . . .
The sticks that budded just when we needed a miracle.
The stone tables of life written with the finger of God.

**Calvin Miller**
Professor of Preaching, Beeson Divinity School

Joy poses the question, "What if God had an attic?" She then delights readers with a thought-provoking journey into such an attic. It is here, in the midst of God's great memories—as captured in Scripture—that we begin to examine our lives and ask, "What are the treasures I'm leaving behind?"

**Robin Jones Gunn**
Author of the best-selling Glenbrooke series
and Christy Miller series.

# Dedication

## For Florene

*who with her siblings endured the stories
behind our heirlooms and who in recent years
designed the house that now holds the family treasures*

# Acknowledgments

I am indebted to singer **Steve Green** whose beautiful rendition of "Find Us Faithful" inspired this book. A verse from the song (words and music by Jon Mohr) speaks of our children sifting through all we've left behind and discovering clues and memories that will become a light for them on their way. It was this concept that led to the project that became *The Treasures We Leave Behind.*

For a dozen books or more I am indebted to **Dave Talbott** and his clear vision for the ministry of writing. As director of the Mount Hermon Christian Writer's Conference, he has provided a lifeline for thousands of writers. For this one, it has made all the difference. Thanks, Dave.

Faithful Woman is an imprint of
Cook Communications Ministries, Colorado Springs, Colorado 80918
Cook Communications, Paris, Ontario
Kingsway Communications, Eastbourne, England

THE TREASURES WE LEAVE BEHIND
© 2001 by Joy P. Gage

First Printing, 2001
Printed in Singapore

1 2 3 4 5 6 7 8 9 10 Printing/Year 05 04 03 02 01

Editor: Afton Rorvik
Cover Design: Smith/Lane Associates
Interior Design: iDesignEtc.
Illustrations: Ron Adair

Published in association with the literary agency of Janet Kobobel Grant, Books & Such, 3093 Maiden Lane, Altadena, CA 91001.

Library of Congress Cataloging-in-Publication Data

Gage, Joy P.
    The treasures we leave behind / Joy P. Gage.
        p. cm.
    Includes bibliographical references.
    ISBN 0-7814-3506-4
    1. Bible stories, English. I. Title.

BS550.2 .G34 2001
220.9'505--dc21

                                                    00-062295

# Contents

# Introduction

MY HUSBAND AND I ARE COMPULSIVE COLLECTORS. OUR HOME IS FILLED with keepsakes that we display in every room. Where other people would have art, we have an ornately framed marriage license that belonged to Ken's deceased parents. Where other people would add wainscoting to their walls, we have added gothic arches salvaged from the balcony of a church built in 1877. From the chipped ironstone plate that hangs in the kitchen to the tiger oak desk that graces the living room, each item reminds us of its original owner, who lived in another place and another time.

To the consternation of our offspring (and our guests, I suspect) everything in the house has a story. Make a comment on any item, and you are sure to hear the story behind it. You may feel you are getting more information than you really want, but I often find myself thinking, *If only these keepsakes could talk, what stories they could tell!*

Perhaps because of our collection, I became fascinated with the artifacts in the Bible. We don't know that any of the men and women in Scripture left behind keepsakes. But if they did, we can be sure what some of them would have been.

What if God had an attic?

The stories in this book highlight artifacts that would surely be found in God's attic if there were such a place.

Some were objects used by God in a miraculous way. All were on the scene when some momentous event took place. And all remind us how God uses that which is common and ordinary to accomplish His uncommon, extraordinary purposes.

༺❀༻

# Chapter One

# The Dome Top Trunk

$\mathcal{B}$ENEATH THE FRONT WINDOWS OF OUR LIVING ROOM SITS AN OLD DOME top trunk. Although expertly refinished by my husband, the trunk shows signs of a long, hard life. The two-inch-wide wooden ribs are nicked, cracked, and incomplete in spots. The tin is broken in places and some of the hardware is missing. Still, it sits there commanding a prominent place in our home and holding one hundred years of secrets.

Of all the artifacts we own, this trunk is the one I treasure the most. We have other items of far greater monetary value, but the trunk reminds me that our greatest treasures are not measured in terms of dollars.

Taped inside the lid is an envelope holding the story behind our trunk. This story awaits coming generations who will sift through what we have left behind. There they will find the account of how an entire family began their spiritual journey.

When I was ten years old my parents sold their few possessions, crammed everything that was left into the trunk, which they had acquired from my grandparents, and moved from their tiny Ozark community to southeastern Arizona.

They moved in order to meet the family's economic, educational, and social needs. (The social need being that my father didn't want his children growing up to marry their cousins.)

With hard work and careful planning, my parents managed to

meet the needs that had propelled their move. In the process, an even greater need was met. In the little desert town, we each found Christ.

The old trunk could hardly withstand a journey today. Still, it serves a useful function for storage and it is an instant conversation starter.

Each time I look at it, I am reminded that the trek west marked a many-sided new beginning for the Pennock family. While the trunk will never travel again, it will continue to symbolize the beginnings of five separate spiritual journeys.

## Rahab's Rope

IF RAHAB LEFT KEEPSAKES, A SCARLET CORD SURELY WAS AMONG THEM. It was only a bit of rope, but it symbolized the beginning of her spiritual journey. Nothing else would have so reminded Rahab of the day her whole life changed.

There was no escaping the hopelessness that hung over Jericho that day. Fear had paralyzed the town—a fear so tangible that one could almost feel it. Everyone knew that the nation of Israel was marching toward Jericho and that very soon Jericho would be conquered by the advancing army.

Still, strictly speaking, it was not the Israelites that Jericho feared. These wandering desert people, just a few decades removed from slavery, posed little threat by themselves. But Israel's God always tipped the balance in their favor. He advanced Israel's armies with a mixture of miracles and mayhem. Every citizen in Jericho knew that Israel's God had already "given Jericho over," and the knowledge of it ripped away each person's courage.

On the day her whole life changed, Rahab awakened to the same hopelessness that paralyzed her fellow citizens. But when two visitors came to her house on the wall, Rahab realized that reprieve from certain doom was possible. She recognized the men as spies from the camp of Israel and suddenly hope stood before her. She determined to throw herself on the mercy of the men and the God they served.

First, she helped the spies by hiding them on her flat roof. When the king's men came to her house searching for the spies, Rahab gave the royal emissaries misleading information and sent them away.

> *On the day her whole life changed, Rahab awakened to the same hopelessness that paralyzed her fellow citizens.*

When it was safe to do so, Rahab went to the roof and, holding nothing back, confided in the spies. She confessed her terror and that of her fellow citizens. They had all heard the reports of how the same God who had dried up the Red Sea over forty years ago had recently destroyed two Amorite kings east of the Jordan.

"Our hearts have melted within us," Rahab acknowledged. Then, under the cover of darkness on her rooftop filled with drying flax, Rahab confessed what she had come lately to believe: "Israel's God is the true God."

Having thus acknowledged the truth, Rahab pleaded with the spies for protection. She asked for their assurance that when they came back with the army, they would rescue her, her parents, her siblings, and all who belonged to them. It seemed a fair request—their kindness in exchange for her kindness. The bargain was struck and the promise was sealed.

"Our lives for yours," they declared. "If a hand is laid on anyone who is in the house with you, his blood will be on our head."

Both the promise and the conditions of it were clear. First, Rahab was not to tell what the spies were doing. Second, she was to bring all those who belonged to her into her house and keep them there. Finally, she was to mark the house by hanging a scarlet cord in her window.

She readily accepted their conditional promise and helped the men escape over the wall from her house. As soon as they were gone, she tied the scarlet cord in her window. She had no idea how

> *One day, the men would return with Israel's army led by Israel's God, and no one would be safe except those inside the house marked by the scarlet cord.*

long the men would be gone or exactly what would happen when they came again. She only knew that Jericho's fate was sealed. One day, the men would return with Israel's army led by Israel's God, and no one would be safe except those inside the house marked by the scarlet cord.

One has to wonder how she managed to convince her family to come to her house when she knew so little about the plan. One also has to wonder whether she repeatedly explained, "I don't know when they're coming back. I only know that when they do, we all have to be in this house." She must have clung to the promise. She must have reminded herself of it many times.

For three days, the men would hide out after leaving Rahab's place. That much she knew because they had agreed on that part of the plan. On the fourth day they would return to Israel's camp. But beyond four days, Rahab could not predict how long she and her family would have to wait.

CRYXWS

The first advance information to reach Jericho was that Israel had crossed the Jordan—an amazing feat since the river was at flood tide. Rumor had it that this God of miracles had pushed back the Jordan, dried out the riverbed, and held the water until all had crossed. Terrified anew, Jericho closed herself up tightly and prepared for a long siege. No one went out and no one came in.

As tension grew in the town, so it must also have grown in the house on the wall. Perhaps Rahab's family could see the smoke from Israel's camp, but they could see little else until the day someone spotted a long column of marching men coming from the direction of Gilgal. The next time the Israelites made camp, they made it just outside Jericho's walls. If it had been nerve-racking for Rahab before, it must have been doubly so once the Israelites arrived at the city walls.

Picture the scene. Rahab's entire extended family living in her home, waiting to be rescued. The house too crowded, the children bored, the adults skeptical, everyone expecting Rahab to have answers to their impatient questions.

How many times did she have to remind her family that she wasn't privy to the plan, she was only the recipient of the promise?

How many times did she check the scarlet cord? Their very lives depended upon that cord. She had to make sure that it remained in place—that some bored niece or nephew did not remove it for a game of jump rope.

The tension must have heightened on the day the marching began. Early that morning, Rahab and her family heard the sound of forty thousand men marching. Trumpets blared at the front of the line, but otherwise it was noticeably quiet. Eerie. Just trumpets and the sound of marching feet. No voices.

Would all of Jericho also have grown quiet, listening and waiting for "the end"?

The army circled the wall, then returned to its camp, leaving the city to wonder once again, *What next?* Jericho could only wait and see.

For six days it was so. The entire army marched around the city with trumpets blaring and voices silent, then returned to camp.

For six days Jericho waited for whatever would come.

On the seventh morning at daybreak the marching began again. But when the usual time had passed, the army did not return to camp. Around and around it went, trumpets blaring at the head, forty thousand men marching in cadence, and silence throughout the ranks.

*She was given a new home, a new identity, and a new place in history.*

Hours passed. Then came a great blare of trumpets, a deafening shout from the soldiers, and suddenly with a jerk and a rumble, the walls of the city gave way and crashed to the ground.

Through the choking dust, Israel's soldiers clambered over the rubble into the city. Everywhere could be heard the sound of running feet, screaming children, and people wailing in the streets. Jericho's doomsday had arrived.

What must Rahab have thought?

What must her family have thought? Did she have to reassure them one last time? Did she have to forcibly keep them inside by standing in front of the door?

What relief she must have felt when two familiar faces appeared at her door. The spies she had hidden on the rooftop stood waiting to escort her and her family to a safe place outside Israel's camp. From that vantage point, they watched as a fire roared through Jericho and destroyed everything in it. Only Rahab and her family escaped.

Rahab was generously rewarded for her kindness to the spies. But her rescue on the day Jericho's walls came crashing down is not the "happy ending" of her story.

Rather, it is the "happy beginning." She was given a new home, a new identity, and a new place in history.

The prostitute who had made her home on the city wall found a new home among the Israelites for the rest of her life.

The woman from Jericho who had been identified by her immoral occupation became a bride in Israel.

As for her place in history, Rahab is one of only three women whose names are mentioned in the genealogy of our Lord.

Rahab married Salmon and gave birth to a son, whom they named Boaz. Boaz grew up and, like his father before him, married a Gentile woman. Her name was Ruth and she bore Boaz a son called Obed. Obed was the father of Jesse, who fathered King David.

We don't know when Rahab died, or whether she left any keepsakes behind. But we do know that her spiritual journey began on the day she declared that Israel's God was the true God—on the day she hung a scarlet cord in her window.

*This story of Rahab's rope is based on Joshua 2—6 and Matthew 1:5-6.*

◁×▷

# Chapter Two

# The Ironstone Plate

*I* HAVE OFTEN SAID THAT WE FURNISHED OUR HOME WITH ONE OLD, chipped, ironstone plate. Although spoken in jest, there is more than a little truth to the statement.

Shortly after Ken and I married, my aunt sent the plate to me with the explanation that it was the last piece from my grandmother's first set of dishes.

At the time, we were living in a logging camp where Ken served as the first resident pastor in the history of the community. We lived in a two-bedroom, unfurnished, knotty pine house with nothing but a bed, a table, a hot plate, and an electric roaster that served as an oven. We had no other appliances for the first thirty days. We had neither curtains for the windows nor anything of beauty to hang on the walls.

My desire to create a cheery home of our sparsely furnished house prompted me to display my grandmother's plate in a prominent place. First, I painted a silhouette of a man and woman on the plate. Then I added their names—Martha and Mike—and the date of their marriage, 1890. The plate has hung in every house in which we have lived since then.

People assumed that anyone who would hang an old, chipped, ironstone plate in the living room must like old things. They began offering their castoffs. Today we have what appears to be a modest collection of antiques, but truthfully, it all began as junk salvaged from other people's attics.

I treasure the plate because it reminds me of my grandmother's story. She was in her early forties when her husband died of pneumonia. Six of their nine children were still at home. Soon afterward one of her married daughters died, leaving an infant girl for Grandma to raise. My aunt told me that when this double tragedy struck, Grandma went up into the attic and "threw herself on the mercy of God." Sensing her own inadequacy, she prayed, "God, I can't do this alone."

There is an old proverb that says, "God couldn't be everywhere at once—that's why He made mothers." The truth is, mothers can't be everywhere at once—that's why we need God. Grandma has been gone for many years, but her plate continues to remind me of mothers everywhere who depend upon God for provision and for the protection of their children.

## The Widow's Oil Cruse

SOMEWHERE IN THE LAND OF ISRAEL THERE ONCE LIVED A WIDOWED mother with a very special oil cruse. I can't imagine that she would have parted with it. Surely that particular oil jar would have remained in her possession for the rest of her natural life. And afterward as her grown sons sifted through what she left behind, they would have recognized the jar's significance. It would have reminded them of the day that God miraculously provided for their family.

This unnamed woman of 2 Kings 4 had known a contented existence with her sons and her husband—a devout man who served as one of the company of prophets. She probably had few concerns other than the sizable debt that her husband was accruing.

Then one tragic day, her husband died and overnight her contentment turned to desperation. She had no means of income. Her food supply ran out. She had nothing with which to pay her husband's debt. If she could not pay it, her sons would be taken as slaves in order to satisfy the creditors.

In his classic devotional book, *Disciplines of Life*, Dr. V. Raymond Edman writes of the discipline of desperation. He acknowledges that in the Christian life there are excruciating moments of despair when life and death hang in the balance, and our only recourse is to cry out to God. If He does not hear us and help us, all is lost.

> *She would perish without help, and she knew of only one place to find that help.*

The biblical widow faced such a moment.

Perhaps in the beginning she drew strength from her own inner resources, developed through years of being a prophet's wife. Perhaps she went up to her rooftop and prayed to God. Perhaps she sought some practical way to remedy the situation. Whatever she might have tried, ultimately this woman realized the situation was out of her control.

Humanly speaking, there was nothing she could do. She would perish without help, and she knew of only one place to find that help. She sought out God's spokesman, the prophet Elisha, and laid her woes before him.

"Your servant, my husband, revered the Lord," she reminded the prophet, "but now his creditor is coming to take my two boys for his slaves."

Contrasting her husband's good record with her own desperate circumstances, she tried to make sense of the situation. He was a good man. He faithfully served the God he loved. "But now . . ."

At best, the two words are a cry for help. At worst, a hint that something is wrong in a world where bad things happen to good people. Why should the family of a faithful prophet suffer such deprivation and anguish?

I wonder whether she experienced a touch of bitterness? Did she question how her husband, who devoted his life to serving God, could be so careless about his own affairs that he would die in debt? Did she blame him for the situation? Did she blame God?

Perhaps. But she also cried out to Him through His prophet, Elisha.

"He's dead," she wailed, and spelled out the details of her triple calamity—widowed, destitute, facing the additional loss of her two sons.

*"Nothing except . . ."*

*The words, the doubt rising out of despair, are all too familiar.*

"What do you have in your house?" the prophet asked.

"Nothing," the widow replied. "Nothing at all, except a little oil."

"Nothing except . . ." The words, the doubt rising out of despair, are all too familiar.

"Nothing except a little oil," she said.

"Nothing except twenty loaves of bread for one hundred people," Elisha's servant told him on a later occasion.

Nothing except ". . . seven loaves and a few small fish," the disciples lamented when Jesus pointed to four thousand hungry people.

In our own desperate situations, we are sometimes forced to recognize that we have no resources left—nothing, that is, except the promises of God.

Annie Johnson Flint could have been describing the widow's situation when she wrote these words:

> When we have exhausted our store of endurance,
> When our strength has failed ere the day is half done,

When we reach the end of our hoarded resources,
Our Father's full giving is only begun.[1]


The widow had come to the very end of her resources when she said to Elisha, "I have nothing except a little oil."

"Go around to all your neighbors," Elisha instructed her. "Ask them for empty jars. Don't ask for just a few. Then go inside and shut the door behind you and your sons. Pour oil into all the jars and as each is filled, put it to one side."

Soon afterward, the widow and her sons could be seen scurrying through the village. Moving from house to house, they asked for any extra jars. We are not told whether the neighbors questioned the little family's sudden need for jars. But there would have been little time given to conversation. Surely the urgency of their situation kept the trio rushing along on their errand.

With arms loaded with jars, they came to their own house and shut themselves inside. A relay began—the mother pouring, the sons fetching empty jars. She poured from her scant supply of olive oil and marveled as it filled the first empty jar. As she set it aside, her son brought another jar and another and another.

One wonders at what point the feeling of desperation began to lift. At what point did the woman begin to believe that everything was going to be all right? . . . Did her facial expression change with each miraculous filling? . . . Were there tears of joy as her eyes caught the eyes of her sons? Did her heart race as she pondered the possibility that these boys would be spared from her husband's creditors? Did she laugh midway through the chore? Did they laugh together as they worked?

Surely the mood in the room had changed by the time the widow bade one of her sons, "Bring me another one," and he replied, "There is not a jar left."

It might seem curious that the woman found it necessary to return to the prophet for further instructions. With all that oil sitting around, would she need someone to tell her what to do next? But, on closer examination, it is clear that Elisha never laid out the whole plan. When the widow hurried away to borrow jars, she

> *With all that oil sitting around, would she need someone to tell her what to do next?*

obeyed God's spokesman one step at a time. After completing all the revealed steps, she left nothing to chance or human wisdom. She sought the prophet's instructions. Only then did she sell the oil, pay her creditors, and buy food for her sons.

For the remainder of her life, the widow's oil cruse must have reminded her of the day God stretched her oil supply. Surely, each time she looked at the jar, she thought of her words to the prophet, "Your servant has nothing at all, except a little oil."

God ignored the "nothing" and multiplied the "except." How could a widowed mother forget such a day?

*This story of the widow's oil cruse was taken from 2 Kings 4:1-7.*

Mr. Peter B. Gage,

I really am afraid I am not qualified to fill the station you would assign me as it deserves to be filled and therefore I cannot conscientiously advise you to cross Lake Erie for the purpose of forming an acquaintance with me, when you can find scores in Michigan far superior to your humble correspondent as well in kindness of disposition as in the art of housekeeping, for I am fearful that I should make rather awkward business of it in a family like yours, as I have ever been in the habit of working when I please and playing when I pleased.

Mary E. Perry

*Chapter Three*

❦

# Letters from the Past

*T*HERE IS NOTHING QUITE LIKE AN OLD LETTER TO GIVE US A SENSE OF our heritage. Initially, the letter may have been little more than an account of the writer's boring daily routine; but after one hundred years, it becomes an important document, revealing life as it was lived in another era.

My cousin Martha has a suitcase full of family letters and miscellaneous papers. Along with documents showing our grandparents' claim to their Ozark farm, she has letters written by a relative who fought in the Civil War. Whenever I visit Martha, I always enjoy pouring over these letters. It gives me a sense of my roots.

In my husband's family, his cousin Betty Anne is the keeper of family historical items. From her we have obtained copies of letters exchanged between Ken's great-grandparents before they were married. They can hardly be called "love letters," but they provide interesting examples of how certain matters were handled at the time.

A widower with four young children to raise, Great-grandfather Peter sought a mother for his children and a companion for himself. Peter's letters are businesslike, blunt, and specific. He explains his situation, his health status, and his comfortable financial position. Great-grandmother Mary's responses are equally blunt, as she explains that she doesn't like housework and is quite accustomed to doing what she pleases when she pleases. They married, nevertheless, and she gave him four more children.

Both our families have letters that document our respective westward migrations. But in my family, the most significant letter concerning our migration is one that was never delivered.

When I was a young child, my father wrote a letter in which he accepted a job offer from a farmer who lived east of us in another state. My parents waited expectantly for the farmer to respond and give all the necessary details about our relocation. Weeks went by and no letter came. One day, after the job opportunity had passed, my father thrust his hand into his jacket pocket and, much to his dismay, discovered the letter he had written to the farmer. His failure to mail the letter changed the course of our lives.

> *But in my family, the most significant letter concerning our migration is one that was never delivered.*

In time, we moved west to Arizona where each of us met Christ. As we reflect on the twists and turns of our family history, we cannot help but believe that God's hand was on our lives even then—that He redirected our paths through such a simple thing as an undelivered letter.

## Paul's Undelivered Letters

WHEN THE APOSTLE PAUL WAS EXECUTED IN ROME, HE PROBABLY LEFT very little behind, save his writing materials. By the time his head fell beneath the sword, Paul had established himself as a writer of letters—

letters to churches he had started

letters to young pastors

letters of reprimand
letters of encouragement
letters of instruction.

Even in prison, he continued his letter writing, and it is not unlikely that an unfinished letter might have been found among his personal effects after he died.

One thing we would not expect to find would be the letters that Paul carried to Damascus at a time when he was yet called Saul of Tarsus. Bent on destroying the church, he had obtained from the high priest letters giving him authority to arrest all those who followed the Way. We don't know what happened to those letters, so important one day, so useless the next. But we do know that they were never delivered.

Saul of Tarsus, the zealous persecutor of the church, hurried along the road to Damascus, confident that nothing could go wrong on his mission. He had made full preparation for his task by securing letters from the high priest, addressed to the synagogues in Damascus. No higher authority was needed to ensure the apprehension and arrest of the followers of Christ.

A great persecution against the church at Jerusalem had scattered the followers throughout Judea and Samaria, and Saul was determined to find them and carry them in chains back to a Jerusalem prison.

He had vivid memories of the day the persecution broke out. On that day, one of the followers of Christ, the stubbornly fearless Stephen, met his death by stoning. Saul had been there—standing by, giving his approval, watching over the cloaks of those who threw the stones. Stephen's body was hardly in the grave before the great persecution broke out. On that same day, Saul began to destroy the church.

A scholarly man by Jewish standards, Saul had studied the Law at the feet of the great Gamaliel. The son of a Pharisee, and a Roman citizen by birth, he was proud of his heritage. Obsessed with destroying anything that threatened Judaism, he soon gained a reputation as a man to be feared. The very mention of his name *Unexpectedly, Saul's persecution of the church ended in a savage burst of light from the sky.* was enough to strike terror into the hearts of those who followed Christ.

By the time Saul set out for Damascus, his murderous threats had marked him as the chief enemy of the faith.

Perhaps his steps quickened as he neared the city. He intended to make prompt work of the matter. With the authority-granting letters, how could anything unexpected thwart his purpose in Damascus?

How, indeed.

Saul had not yet reached the city when, unexpectedly, his persecution of the church ended in a savage burst of light from the sky.

Blinded by its brilliance, he fell to the ground as a voice spoke to him. "Saul, Saul, why do you persecute Me?"

"Who are You, Lord?" Saul asked.

"I am Jesus, whom you are persecuting," the voice replied.

A few miles short of his destination, still carrying letters allowing him to destroy the church, the zealous persecutor listened to the One he had persecuted.

"Get up and go into the city, and you will be told what you must do," the voice commanded.

Obediently, Saul stood up and, still blinded, allowed his companions to lead him by the hand. They brought him to a house on Straight Street where he waited for three days.

Three days with no sight.

Seventy-two hours of stumbling and fumbling.

Four thousand, three hundred and twenty minutes in which to analyze the encounter on the road.

He neither ate nor drank.

He spent his time praying to the God whose church he had so recently tried to destroy.

Meanwhile, across town, a disciple named Ananias had a frightening vision in which the Lord told him to go to the house of Judas and ask for a man from Tarsus named Saul.

Saul's reputation had preceded him. Ananias knew all about this man—the harm he had done to believers in Jerusalem, the reason he had come to Damascus, the letters he carried on his person. Terrified, Ananias questioned the Lord's directive.

He could hardly believe God's response.

"Go . . . for he is My chosen instrument to carry My name before the Gentiles, and kings, and the children of Israel. I will show him how much he must suffer for My name."

Could it be true?

Could this one who had purposed to destroy the church now be charged with building it up?

Could the one who had inflicted suffering upon believers now be called to suffer for the cause?

One wonders how Ananias felt as he went to find Saul. Was he apprehensive? Reluctant? Curious? Whether he went fearlessly, or haltingly, he obediently delivered God's message.

According to God's instructions, Ananias laid hands on Saul so that he could "see again and be filled with the Holy Spirit."

The former persecutor's new life began roughly.

He preached in the synagogues and left his audiences gaping as he proclaimed that Jesus was the Son of God.

Wasn't this the man who had raised havoc in Jerusalem among the believers of such dogma?

Wasn't this the man who had come to Damascus to arrest all such believers?

So effective was Saul in his reversed role that the baffled Jews conspired to kill him. Day and night they watched the city gates in order to apprehend him. But the disciples, Saul's new brothers in the faith, took him by night and lowered him in a basket through an opening in the wall.

Retracing his journey, Saul returned to Jerusalem where more problems awaited him. There, the terror-stricken disciples rejected Saul's attempts to join them. Only after Barnabas brought him to the apostles and vouched for Saul did the believers receive him into their number.

For a brief time Saul moved about freely, preaching what he had come lately to believe. But in Jerusalem as in Damascus, his life was threatened. This time, when the disciples helped him escape, they sent him down to Tarsus.

With Saul's conversion, the church began to enjoy a season of peace. In time, Saul of Tarsus became known as Paul the Apostle.

A more zealous man than the Apostle Paul is not seen in the Scriptures. The zealot bent on destroying the church became an equally zealous witness to the claims of Christ.

The impact of this chosen instrument can hardly be measured. Just as God had told Ananias, Paul did become a great instrument who spoke to Gentiles, to kings, and to Israel.

And just as God had said, Paul did suffer much for the cause of Christ. He was flogged numerous times, shipwrecked three times, stoned and left for dead on one occasion, and continually endangered by enemies and elements alike.

A prolific letter writer, Paul wrote continually to churches and to young pastors. Some of his most encouraging letters were written from a prison cell as he waited for Rome to decide his fate.

His last letter, written from prison, was addressed to Timothy, whom he loved as a son.
Written to encourage the young pastor to stand firm in his faith, the letter reveals Paul's unique perspective in the face of death.

> *The zealot bent on destroying the church became an equally zealous witness to the claims of Christ.*

He had purpose and peace amid pain and suffering.

He determined to endure until he was taken from this world.

He acknowledged the cruel reality of his situation, but he contrasted it with the reality of his hope.

He acknowledged his chains but declared that God's Word was unchained.

Secular historian Will Durant states that for a century after Paul's death he was almost forgotten. "But when the first generations of Christianity had passed away, and the oral tradition of the apostles began to fade, and a hundred heresies disordered the Christian mind, the epistles of Paul provided the framework for a stabilizing system of belief that united the scattered congregations into a powerful Church."[1]

Throughout history, the letters of Paul, with the rest of Scripture, have been threatened with destruction. But no force has proved able to destroy what God deems indestructible. The letters, divinely inspired and divinely preserved, remain for our learning today.

Curious, isn't it? God stopped a man who was carrying letters of authority to destroy the church, then He inspired that same man to write letters that would strengthen the church.

We are left with this picture of letters in the hand of God. On the one hand He determined that certain letters would be undelivered and through that act, He redirected the life of His chosen servant, Saul.

On the other hand God determined that Paul's letters (as well as all of Scripture) will be undestroyed, and through those letters He continues to direct, or redirect, the lives of believers everywhere.

*This story of Paul's undelivered letters was taken from Acts 8:1-3; 9:1-31.*

# Chapter Four

# The Oak Secretary

*O*UR GIRLS WERE QUITE SMALL WHEN KEN'S MOTHER GAVE US AN ANTIQUE oak secretary. We are the third generation to own this family heirloom, and we expect to pass it on to a daughter one day.

The value of our heirloom is increased by the fact that the original round glass door is still intact. We have taken great pains to protect that door. We never allowed toys in the same room for fear one would be hurled across the room and smash the glass. We trained little hands to avoid touching the glass. We often positioned ourselves in front of the door as we managed the traffic flow of a room full of guests. Each time we moved, we waited anxiously to see that our heirloom oak secretary arrived safely. I remember yet how I gasped when two movers grabbed the piece and one proceeded to back out the front door and almost fell off the porch.

Our middle daughter, now a designer, was in the fourth grade when she first came to appreciate the beauty of the oak secretary. Often, she could be found looking at it intently. One day she said rather wistfully, "Can I have this when you're through with it?" It has had her name on it ever since.

I have distinct memories of my mother-in-law's words the day she gave us this piece of furniture. She felt compelled to tell us that we should take care of it because a neighbor had recently told her it was valuable. She even told us the amount of money the man thought the piece would bring. (A paltry sum compared to its current worth.)

I will always believe that her admonition came, in part, because we had not taken good care of a dresser she had given to us on a previous occasion. It was a beautiful old-fashioned oak dresser that we promptly "modernized" by cutting off the legs and painting it yellow.

I cringe at the thought of that today. I also regret the fact that we lost my grandmother's cast iron waffle iron and that an antique Royal Doulton plate was broken in our last move. It's not that I give a high priority to things. It's just that I don't believe we ever truly own family heirlooms. They are more like a trust to be cared for and handed down to the next generation.

To treat fine heirlooms carelessly is much the same as to squander one's inheritance. Jesus told a story about a young man who probably had not learned that it is not a good idea to cut off the legs of an antique dresser and paint it yellow. He was not the sort to value family heirlooms. In fact, we may safely assume that he would have sold every one he could find and used the money to gratify his wildest desires.

⌒⌒⌒

# A Ring for the Prodigal Child

JESUS WAS A MASTER STORYTELLER. HE TOLD STORIES TO MAKE A POINT.

The antagonist in one of His best-known parables was a young man who had much more regard for his immediate needs and for his own pleasure than for the family name or the family fortune.

The antagonist has an older brother, also a main character, who exhibits behavior that is symptomatic of his birth order. He is devoted to duty and consciously concerned about pleasing his father. Unfortunately, none of this rubs off on the younger brother.

As the plot unfolds in Jesus' story, the younger brother assesses his situation and decides that there is a great deal more to see and experience in the world. In the opening scene, he persuades his father to give him his inheritance early. With fortune in hand, the young man immediately sets off to explore parts unknown.

He has a great time indulging his every whim and experiencing everything there is to experience. He assumes that his resources will last forever, but his appetite for wine, women, and wild parties proves to be greater than his inherited fortune.

> *One morning as he shakes the latest hangover out of his head, he realizes that he is destitute.*

One morning as he shakes the latest hangover out of his head, he realizes that he is destitute.

At this point in his story, Jesus creates tension by showing that things get a lot worse before they get better. Our main character takes a job feeding the pigs of some farmer in the far away country. (A rather nasty job for one of his heritage.)

In a great high point of the story, we see the young man so hungry that he is tempted to eat that which he feeds to the pigs. It is this scene that leads to resolution. The young man comes to his senses. "What am I doing here?" ("Starving to death" would be the appropriate answer.) This is the moment of truth for our character. This moment resolves itself in a change of goals.

"Why should I stay here?" he asks himself. "My father's servants have plenty to eat."

So we have this scene where the character makes a second life-changing decision. (The first was when he decided to take what belonged to him and spend it on whatever gave him pleasure.) He now realizes that his inheritance is gone forever, but perhaps he need not be hungry. He will return to his father's home, beg forgiveness, and ask for a place among the servants.

The protagonist in Jesus' story is a wise father who knows the value of reaching out to less than perfect sons. Jesus portrayed him as a loving man who watched every day for the return of his prodigal child.

In an emotional homecoming scene, the father makes it very easy for the foolish son to seek forgiveness. He welcomes the boy, gives him a cloak, and puts a ring on his finger. Then he orders the servants to fire up the barbecue and kill a fat calf.

But the story doesn't end yet.

Enter the older son. In a dramatic scene, Jesus shows the first-born son coming in from the field. He hears all the music and dancing and corners the nearest servant.

"What's going on?" he asks.

"Your brother has come home, and your father has killed a calf because he has him back safe and sound."

At this the older brother grows angry. He pouts and refuses to join the party.

The wise father extends the same love to both sons. He had waited for the prodigal; now he seeks out the pouter.

The ensuing scene represents the whole point of Jesus' story. (He was making the point to the Pharisees who criticized Him for keeping company with sinners.) Through some tense dialogue, we learn the reason for the older son's objection to the celebration.

> *The protagonist in Jesus' story is a wise father who knows the value of reaching out to less than perfect sons.*

"Look how long I've slaved away for you, and you never once killed so much as a goat for me and my friends. But when my low-life brother comes home, you barbeque a calf for him."

The patient father explains about the feast. It was not given as a reward for the foolish son. Nor was the calf killed so much for the son as for the father. The father had thought his son to be dead. Finding him alive called for a real celebration.

A line of the father's dialogue gives us an idea of what might have happened in later years. "Everything I have is yours," the father tells the older son.

So we know that while the younger son was forgiven and even restored to his father's love (he didn't make a servant of him), the consequences of his foolishness remained. His inheritance was gone. There was nothing to be done about it. Everything that was left belonged to the older son.

✿

The story of the prodigal son is as relevant today as when it was first told by the master storyteller. But it is most palatable in the setting of the sanctuary when the minister is preaching his three-point sermon on Luke 15.

In real life the story can get messy.

Young man turns his back on his parents.

Young man messes up his life and breaks his parents' hearts.

Young man learns his lesson the hard way and seeks reconciliation with his parents.

How will the story end? Will a fatted calf celebration follow?

Maybe. But it takes more than a calf. It takes forgiveness.

Forgiving a prodigal child has never been easy. Parents are human. Humans quickly tire of rejection. They tire of ill treatment. They feel used when love is taken for granted and never reciprocated. But if there is to be a celebration, there must be forgiveness.

Asking for forgiveness has never been easy. The father in Jesus' story understood that. He ran to meet his returning son, making it easy for the boy to pour out his repentance.

Jesus never told a sequel to this story. (Obviously, He did not work for earthly editors.) But we can imagine different plot lines. Sibling rivalry could have escalated into a real conflict, tearing the family apart. Or the poverty-stricken younger brother, forgiven and restored, could lead the way in reconciling with his rich older brother. Or the younger brother could gain a fortune by the work of his hands.

Whether he died a rich or a poor man, the younger brother would likely leave behind one small treasure that meant more to him than any thing he owned—a ring that his father had given him.

> *Forgiving a prodigal child has never been easy. Parents are human. Humans quickly tire of rejection. They tire of ill treatment.*

The ring provided a constant reminder that he had been forgiven by his father and restored to the status of a son. It was a symbol of a father's love, a link to the day that the prodigal child came home and the father celebrated.

*This story about a ring for the prodigal child is based on Luke 15:11-32.*

*Chapter Five*

❦

# A Handmade Baby Dress

*I*N OUR GUEST ROOM HANGS A BABY DRESS MADE OF PARACHUTE SILK. IT
is completely handstitched down to the French seams that were necessary to prevent fraying. The scalloped collar, miniature pockets,
and tiny puffed sleeves are carefully embroidered in blue. It is one
of three lovingly crafted dresses made by my mother for our infant
daughters.

Mother was a self-taught seamstress and did not always excel
at the job. But she would try anything. She once made a fringed
leather jacket from a deer hide. My wedding gown was one of the
finest examples of her sewing. So were the dresses she made for our
baby girls.

My daughters have no strong memories of my mother. She died
when they were very young. I am sorry that they did not get to know
this woman who had such a strong spiritual influence on my life.

Spiritually speaking, my mother, my sister, my brother, and I
were all the same age because we came to Christ at the same time.
My earliest memories of our "new life" is of my mother sitting on
the edge of the bed, surrounded by my siblings and me, reading the
Bible with the weekly Sunday School lesson. Since she had no background, she depended upon the materials furnished her, but she lost
no time getting into the Word and training her children to do the
same.

From the beginning my mother had a consistent prayer life. First she prayed for my father, the one remaining member of the family who had not found Christ. By the time he became a believer, we children were all in high school and she began to pray for God's direction in our lives.

I think my mother's prayers were specific. She desired her children to serve God if God so willed, but she never talked about that to anyone but God. If the subject came up about service for God as opposed to some secular field of work, she never

> *In one short sentence, she could say enough to keep me thinking for several weeks.*

pressured us. But she had a way about her. In one short sentence, she could say enough to keep me thinking for several weeks. The fact that she would say it and then drop the subject unnerved me. It made me think all the more.

In the last years of her life, Mother was led to pray for my father's spiritual growth. She confided in me, "I prayed, 'Lord, bring my husband closer to You even if it takes me.'" She died a year later of colon cancer. In the mysterious ways of God, my father experienced his greatest spiritual growth following Mother's death.

I regret that she did not live to see the publication of my first book. I know that, in part, everything I have accomplished has been her legacy. She always believed in me, and she was my greatest prayer warrior until the day she died.

When my daughters look at the dresses made for them by the grandmother about whom they have few memories, I hope that they will remember this one thing: she was a woman of prayer and her greatest prayer efforts were on behalf of her family.

# Samuel's Robes

IF I WERE HANNAH, I KNOW WHAT I WOULD HAVE LEFT BEHIND. I WOULD have left a collection of children's robes of various sizes, all worn by my eldest son while he was growing up. I don't think I would have allowed any of my other five children to wear the outgrown robes that I brought home each year after we made our pilgrimage to Jerusalem. I would have kept the robes in a private place where I could look at them and think about the son who had been with me for such a short time before I entrusted him to the care of the priest at Jerusalem.

On days when I awakened with an empty feeling, wishing that I could hug my son close to me, I would have pressed the latest outgrown robe to my cheek and sighed because my Samuel was growing up so quickly.

I would have paused to give thanks that my sovereign God had chosen to answer my prayer—that even though my son was far away, he was my son. He was the fruit of my womb.

I think that as I stitched a new robe each year I would have prayed for this special child who had been given to me when God ended my years of barrenness. I would have kept his outgrown robes until the day I died.

Hannah ached for a child.

She ached to the very core of her being to fold her arms around the issue of her own womb. The deep pain caused by her barren state was intensified by the taunting of her husband's other wife, who had many children. The pain was not alleviated by the fact that Elkanah went out of his way to show Hannah special consideration.

"Am I not better to you than ten sons?" he asked. But his words did not relieve the ache in Hannah's heart.

It was a woman kind of ache, a missing piece of life for which a husband's love could not fully compensate. Hannah was caught in the grip of a human desire

> *It was a woman kind of ache, a missing piece of life for which a husband's love could not fully compensate.*

known only to barren women who never get through a day without thinking about the child who isn't there. Hannah thought of little else. She couldn't eat. Her face mirrored her pain.

In her desperation, she turned to God.

It happened on their annual visit to the tabernacle. While there, Hannah prayed for a child. So great was her burden that she could not utter the words. Her lips moved in rhythm with the pain in her heart, but no sound came forth.

From his post nearby, Eli, the aging priest, observed Hannah. He rebuked her, accusing her of drunkenness.

Some women would have lashed out. "You don't have any idea of who I am or what is going on with me!"

Some would have retreated, thinking the accusation unworthy of a response.

It would have been easy simply to go away because this man of God showed a complete lack of understanding of the situation. If the spiritual mentor made a judgment before getting the facts, what hope did one have?

But Hannah wasn't looking to Eli for affirmation or for help. She put her confidence in the Lord and in that frame of mind she explained to Eli the emotions (if not the facts) of her situation.

"I am a deeply troubled woman. I have not been drinking. I was pouring out my soul to the Lord. Don't take me for a wicked woman.

I've been praying out of my great anguish and sorrow."

Her frank response bought Eli's understanding and blessing. "Go in peace, and may God grant you whatever it is that you have asked of Him."

She went away feeling better. Her appetite returned, her countenance brightened.

The next day they returned to their home at Ramah. Within the year Hannah gave birth to a son. She did not go again to the tabernacle for at least three years.

That Hannah was a woman of deep spiritual understanding is evidenced by her actions both before and after the birth of her child. Before his birth, when her burden became greater than she could bear, she sought the only possible help—God Himself. Afterward, she demonstrated a perfect understanding of the balance between maternal and spiritual responsibility. First, she gave her son a mother's tender care. Then, in the course of time, she weaned him and took him to be left in the care of Eli, the priest.

At the tabernacle in Jerusalem, Hannah praised God for the fact that He had miraculously answered her prayer and lifted her up in the face of her enemies. She spent fully half of her prayer extolling the sovereignty of God who sends death or makes alive, who sends poverty or wealth, who both humbles and exalts. Her prayer reveals her deep personal understanding of the sovereignty of God.

We see that sovereignty in the birth of Samuel, but we may overlook that same sovereignty at work in Samuel's life. Consider the facts of his childhood. His mother placed him in the care of an aging priest who was half-blind, a weak and ineffective father to his own sons, and a negligent spiritual leader. There was nothing to recommend him as one to bring up a child who had been dedicated to God. But a sovereign God had plans for this child, and He made up for the lacks in Eli, the priest.

One year on their annual trek to Jerusalem, Hannah learned that God had revealed Himself to her son. Such a rare thing in Israel. For in this time when the nation was ruled sporadically by judges and every man lived by his own code, God had not made many revelations. But He revealed Himself to Samuel. In the middle of the night God had called. Eventually, at Eli's urging, Hannah's son responded to the call saying, "Speak Lord, for your servant is listening." And indeed, the Lord had spoken.

What a revelation it was.

Young boy. Old priest.

First revelation to the young boy. Last warning to the old priest.

A revelation that would make the ears of everyone who heard it tingle.

God declared it was time to bring judgment against Eli's family forever. Samuel understood. But Samuel was afraid to tell Eli. He did not know that God had already spoken to Eli, had already explained that because Eli knew about the contemptible actions of his sons and did not restrain them, God would see to it that there would never be an old man in Eli's line. His descendants would die in the prime of their lives.

Samuel was afraid to tell Eli about God's revelation to him. He lay down until morning and surely spent a sleepless night, hoping that Eli would forget to ask about the incident. To Eli's credit, he not only insisted that Samuel tell him all that the Lord had said, but he responded with, "He is the Lord, let Him do what is good in His eyes." At least this one lesson from the old priest prepared Samuel for the work God called him to do.

As Samuel came into adulthood and became God's man (the last of the judges, the first of the prophets), Israel experienced many more revelations from God. When Samuel became the first prophet in Israel, it was said of him that none of his words failed. Whatever he spoke by God's revelation always came to pass. He was the bridge between the old and the new. He lived to see the kingdom of Israel established. He anointed the first king and mourned over Saul's failure until the day he died. He also anointed David, the king through whom God chose to bring the line of the Messiah.

Humanly speaking, Hannah should never have had this child. Humanly speaking, Samuel, under the care of Eli, should never have developed as a spiritual and moral leader. There had to be divine intervention in both cases. That Samuel became such a servant of God can only be attributed to the fact that the same God who gave Hannah a son also cared for that son.

While it has been customary to call upon Hannah's experience when "dedicating" a child to the Lord, I stumble over all the facts of the case. I have to ask myself what mother would emulate her action in turning over her son to a man like Eli, not a wicked man but one who turned a blind eye to wickedness. A well-intentioned leader with little influence over any action other than his own.

I have to ask myself how it is that a young boy with such a lack of role models actually developed into the kind of man that Samuel became.

I can only conclude that Samuel was called of God and that it was God, not Hannah, who determined the role Samuel played. As for Hannah, her story isn't so much about a mother's act of dedicating her child as it is about the prayer life of one woman who believed in a God who is sovereign.

*This story about Samuel's robes is taken from 1 Samuel 1–3.*

# Chapter Six

# The Stone Butter Churn

Y STONE BUTTER CHURN WAS TWICE RESCUED. ONCE FROM MY grandmother's smokehouse, and once from my mother's storage shed.

We children were seldom allowed in Grandma's smokehouse. When we were, it was under the watchful eye of an adult or my young uncle who was almost an adult. I don't recall a time when the building was ever used for smoking meat. In my memory, the smoke-house was always a place where Grandma stored her cast-off treasures—mostly household items that she no longer used. Just inside the door, attached close to the door frame, was a coffee grinder that I longed to see someone use. Grandma made her morning coffee from a rich brown ground substance that came in a red paper bag. I couldn't imagine what one would do with a "coffee grinder."

High above my head, just a few feet below the ceiling, some boards had been installed as makeshift shelves. Even by craning my neck I could not guess what treasures were held there. But tucked away in one of the corners was the stone churn, still smelling faintly of sour cream. I'm sure someone had to explain to me what it was because long before I came along, Grandma had discarded it in favor of a more modern glass "daisy churn."

Grandma couldn't bring herself to throw away the old stone churn. But she left it behind, along with whatever other treasures the smokehouse held, when they sold out and followed us to Arizona. Later, on a visit to her former home, my mother acquired the stone churn from the new owners. She carried it back to Arizona and put it in her storage shed, where it sat until after I married. One day I suggested to her that the churn would look better in my living room then in her shed, and she promptly gave it to me.

Today it sits atop the Hoosier cabinet in our dining area, a constant reminder of my maternal grandparents. They were city people who tried to make a go of it on a sixty-five-acre Ozark farm. According to family legend, Grandpa bought the farm, site unseen, and when my mother (then about thirteen) first saw her "new home in the country," she

> *If you could change something, there was no need to cry. If you couldn't change it, it wouldn't do any good to cry.*

burst into tears. No doubt the rustic, two-room log cabin was a great contrast to the home from which they moved. But Grandma was never one to cry. If you could change something, there was no need to cry. If you couldn't change it, it wouldn't do any good to cry.

Transforming her cabin into a lovely home was but one of many challenges Grandma faced on their farm. The Great Depression, followed by a devastating drought that sucked the life from the land, thwarted their plans for a better life in the country. My father, a great admirer of his mother-in-law, credits Grandma with pulling the family through. In the midst of a time of hunger and leanness, Grandma continually encouraged the family by saying, "Some day we'll all look back and laugh about this."

They did.

Years later over a bountiful Thanksgiving dinner in Arizona, the adults reminisced about the hard, lean years and Grandma's words. I began to look at Grandma in a new way that day. In the years that followed, I came to understand that whatever other memories the family would have of her, Grandma would be remembered best as the matriarch who "preached" a message of hope in the midst of the darkest of times.

✿

# The Woman at the Well

THE WOMAN SAUNTERED ALONG WITH HER WATER POT ON HER HEAD, HER robe flapping about her ankles, and her eyes avoiding those she met on the path to the town well. Not that those she chanced to meet would be apt to stop and chat. She had a reputation in this Samaritan village. She had been married five times already (two more than the law allowed), and she was currently living with a man who had not bothered to marry her. There were no secrets in the village, and the woman was accustomed to being ignored.

Arriving at the ancient well, she spied a stranger there—a man. She looked away. Certainly she would not expect an exchange of greeting here because men did not speak to women in public. (In private, well, that was another matter.) But to her great surprise, he spoke to her.

*Jewish,* she thought. His speech left no doubt of it, and that fact surprised her all the more. The Jews had no dealings with the Samaritans. Yet here he was, a Jewish man asking something of her, a Samaritan woman.

"Give me water to drink," he asked.

So surprised and curious was she that she ignored the man's request and asked him to explain himself. "How is it that you being a Jew asked a drink of me, a woman of Samaria? You Jews don't mix with Samaritans."

His reply raised her curiosity even more. "If you knew the gift of God and who it is that asks a drink of you, you would have asked of Him and He would have given you living water."

She wasn't sure of his meaning. But of one thing she was sure. He had nothing with which to draw the water so how could he give her any—living or otherwise?

"The well is very deep," she told him. "You have nothing to draw it with so how can you give me this living water?" It occurred to her that if someone could draw living water from the depths of the well with no vessel at hand, then he would have to be even greater than Jacob who dug the well. She boldly suggested that to him.

"Whoever drinks of this water will thirst again," he told her. "But whoever drinks of the water that I shall give him shall never thirst again, but the water that I give will be a well of water springing up into everlasting life."

His words gave her hope. If she didn't thirst, there would be no need to come to the well every day. There would be no need to

*"Sir, give me this water so that I won't thirst again, and I won't ever have to come here to draw water again."*

draw from this well that was so much deeper than that of other villages. There would be no need to walk along the path, smarting under the gaze of her accusers.

"Sir, give me this water so that I won't thirst again, and I won't ever have to come here to draw water again."

He looked her in the eyes and made his own request. "Go get your husband and come here."

"I don't have a husband," she replied. She spoke the truth—but not all of it.

To her great surprise, he filled in the details. "You have well said that you have no husband. You have had five already, and the man you are living with is not your husband. So you have spoken truthfully."

Others in the village were well aware of the facts of her life. But this man was a stranger. How could he know? "Sir, I perceive that you are a prophet," she said. How else could she explain that he knew all about her?

She didn't want to discuss her life. It made her uncomfortable. Her conscience troubled her much of the time, and she didn't need some stranger reminding her of all the wrong turns she had taken. Better to change the subject. Better to bring up some debated question to divert his attention.

"Our fathers worshiped on this mountain," she said. "But you Jews say that Jerusalem is the place where people ought to go to worship."

He made several authoritative statements in response: the Samaritans did not know what they worshiped; the Jews knew what they worshiped; salvation was by the Jews; but as far as where to worship, a time was coming when all true worshipers would worship God in spirit; not the place of worship but the heart of the worshiper would be important.

Confusion mounted along with the woman's curiosity. Of one thing she could be sure. One day Messiah would come. She ventured an opinion. "I know that Messiah is coming—the Christ—and when He comes, He will tell us all things."

"I am He," He told her.

What had begun as an ordinary water collection foray had turned into a series of surprises. First this Jewish man asked her for water. Next He gave every evidence of being a prophet. Then He claimed that He was the Messiah. Still reeling from their conversation, the woman looked up to see more men coming to the well, and for what purpose she could not imagine. They had no water jugs and in any case, men did not draw household water.

Her unvoiced questions were soon answered as it became apparent that these men were traveling with the man who claimed to be the Messiah. Uncomfortable in their presence, she hurried away. In her eagerness to be gone, she forgot her water pot.

In the village once more, she said to the first group of people that she saw, "Come see a man who told me everything I ever did. This can't be the Messiah, can it?"

With a past like hers, who would listen, or who would believe her if she said she had found the Messiah? But to announce to the village people that she had met a man who told her everything she ever did—that

> *With a past like hers, who would listen, or who would believe her if she said she had found the Messiah?*

got their attention. It might have struck terror into the hearts of a few. Perhaps some of those to whom she spoke had shared a part of her past. Did this man know about them as well?

The woman's announcement was enough to convince the villagers to check it out. They hurried away to the well to meet a man called Jesus. They intended to discover for themselves who He really was.

The Samaritan men pleaded with Jesus to stay with them and teach them. Never mind that no self-respecting Jew would have stayed in the region of Samaria. He stayed for two days and taught the seeking Samaritans.

Many of the people of the village believed in Jesus after that. Ultimately they went to the woman and said, "Now we believe, not because of what you said, but because we have heard Him with our own ears, and we know that He is the Christ, the Savior of the world."

Although the village people ultimately believed because of their own encounter with Christ, the testimony of the woman is credited with leading to their conversion.

She was an unlikely evangelist at best with her mistake-riddled past. A sin-riddled past, if the rumors were true.

She was acutely aware of her own lack of worth and her inability to escape the bitter facts that defined her life.

She likely bought the village version of who she was.

She was doubtlessly a bit uncomfortable with God. No matter how she told herself that she was a victim, that she had been used by the men in her life, she could not completely rid herself of those guilt twinges. She could not quite look herself in the brass mirror and feel good about what she saw.

She pretended indifference to the criticism of the village people. She pretended it so long that she became indifferent. Almost.

Her heart grew colder and then turned to stone. Almost.

She wished so much for change but concluded it was impossible. Almost.

How could such a one introduce others to God?

Of course, she first had to meet Him. And when she met the Messiah, it changed her life. She went away eager to tell others. There was no pretense there. By her statement, she freely admitted that her life had been less than exemplary. But the past wasn't the point. The point was that she had met the Messiah.

By her simple testimony, the people of the village met Him also.

I wonder when she retrieved her water jug. I like to imagine that it could have ended up in the local museum as an important part of the town's history. I like to think that it would have reminded the townspeople of the day that the Jewish Jesus came to their Samaritan town and taught them for two whole days.

I like to think that ever afterward, the men of the village looked at this woman in a different way.

*This story of the woman at the well was taken from John 4.*

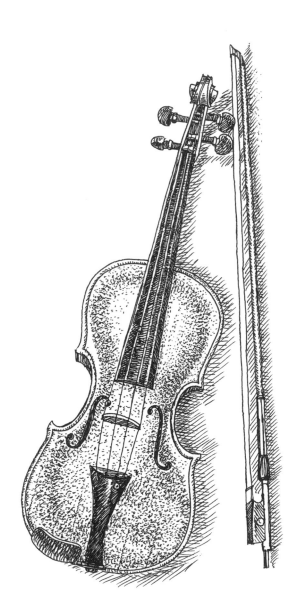

~~×~~

# Chapter Seven

# The Fiddle

 $\mathcal{M}$ Y NINETY-THREE-YEAR-OLD FATHER GAVE ME HIS FIDDLE SEVERAL YEARS ago. Since I don't play it, he has continued to keep it with him because, in spite of his arthritic hands, he still enjoys playing it. He complains that his hands won't allow him to play as he once did. About once a week, he threatens to lay it down and never take it up again. But the music is in his blood, and he cannot stop for long. Nor can we imagine him without his fiddle.

He is a prize winning fiddler who comes from a family of fiddlers. I have a favorite photo of him playing his father's fiddle, an instrument that has been in the Pennock family for well over one hundred years.

In Dad's large and gregarious family there were always a number of fiddlers and guitarists to provide the entertainment at family gatherings, and for many years my father was the fiddler of choice.

Appropriately, when we moved to Arizona, the family gathered at my uncle's for one last night of listening to the music that so identified our family. It would be five years before we next gathered in family reunion. By that time my fifteen-year-old cousin Peggy was inching toward her own place among the family fiddlers.

They begin early. Dad played for his first square dance at age fourteen. When he was eighteen, he played for a square dance held at a hastily constructed floor in a grove of maple trees. He was distracted that night by the appearance of a fifteen-year-old little blond-haired girl. She married him a year later.

The early years of my parents' marriage were set in bleak times, but I have no memory of the leanness. I only remember the music. Each night I fell asleep to the sound of my father's fiddle.

There is a great deal of comfort, even for a child, to be derived from music. Music can be soothing and uplifting, contemplative and celebrative. It has been called the language of the soul.

David, the sweet singer of Israel, spoke that language. He played a stringed instrument—the harp. His music provided background for contemplation as he spent many hours in the field with the sheep.

In time, it also soothed the heart of a troubled king.

# David's Harp

WHEN DAVID THE KING DIED, I WOULD GUESS THAT NOT FAR FROM HIM stood a harp that had been with him most of his life. From his youth, David was identified with this instrument.

One can easily picture this youngest son of Jesse tending his father's sheep—alone day after day in the pastures. While the sheep grazed, David played his harp. It was an instrument of praise that drew him closer to the God whom he praised.

"The Lord is my shepherd," he sang, "I shall not want." This much-loved psalm transports us to tranquil scenes and everlasting provision. But all was not tranquil in the pastures where David spent his days. There were times when he was forced to lay aside his harp and defend the sheep. When his shepherding tasks became too great for him, he sought divine strength and God enabled him to kill the wild animals that attacked the sheep. David found that strength sufficient, and he never doubted its source.

David's comings and goings were entirely at his father's bidding. If Jesse wanted David in the fields, David went. If his father called him from the fields, David came.

But first, he made arrangements for someone to care for the sheep.

On one such day David was called from the pastures and when he arrived at his father's house, he saw that a feast was in progress. All his older brothers were there and Samuel the prophet had come. Something momentous was happening and, as it turned out, David was at the center. The prophet anointed him as the future king of Israel, and from that day forward the Spirit of the Lord came upon the young shepherd boy.

> *Something momentous was happening and, as it turned out, David was at the center.*

On another day, David was called from the pasture. This time, a messenger from King Saul awaited. The king sought a harpist and David had been recommended.

The king was in trouble. The Spirit of God had left him and an evil spirit tormented him. At times he was out of control, his actions completely under the influence of the evil spirit. Hopefully, the music would soothe him.

David played for the troubled king. His music soothed Saul and restored a semblance of peace to his soul. Saul made an arrangement with Jesse. David would remain in the service of the king. David became an armor bearer, and he continued to play as needed. But he went back and forth between the palace of the king and the pastures of his father.

In the pastures he continued to play his harp and sing praises to the great omnipotent God of Israel.

A third time he was called from the pastures. This time, Jesse was concerned about his three older sons who were fighting in Saul's army. Jesse wondered how his sons fared. He loaded a donkey with cheese, bread, and wine and told David to take the supplies to the battlefront.

He arrived at the battle scene as the army was making its line. After dutifully depositing the food supplies, David rushed to the front to check on the situation. Saul's army held its line at the top of a hill. Across the valley on a facing hill, the Philistine army closed ranks.

Suddenly a giant of a man stood center front and shouted across the valley. Over nine feet tall, he wore a bronze helmet and armor. A bronze javelin hung on his back. "Send me a man and let me fight with him," he taunted. "If he wins, we will be your subjects. If I win, you will be our subjects."

As David watched, the Israelites ran in fear. Through snatches of conversation, he learned the details of the situation. This giant of a man had been coming out every morning for forty days. He fearlessly defied Israel. King Saul was willing to reward greatly any man who would fight the godless Philistine. To such a man would be given great wealth, the hand of Saul's daughter in marriage, and tax exemption for his family.

David listened and asked questions. In fact he asked the question that the terror-stricken Israelites had ignored for forty days. "Who is this uncircumcised Philistine that he should defy the armies of the living God?"

Obviously, David had a different perspective on the battle scene. His harp-playing days in the pastures of his father had given him an intimate knowledge of the God whom the giant dared to defy.

When Goliath roared, "Send a man to fight with me," Saul's army saw a man who stood a full three feet taller than the tallest of the king's troops. David saw a mere man who dared to challenge an omnipotent God. What chance could Goliath have?

David's boldness angered his older brother Eliab.

"Why have you come here?" Eliab demanded. "With whom did you leave the sheep?" Angrily, he accused David, "I know how conceited you are and how wicked your heart is. You came down here only to watch the battle."

"Now what have I done?" David countered. "Can't I even speak?"

Eliab surely knew that David never left the sheep unattended, that he never left the pasture except at their father's command. Perhaps Eliab's attitude could be explained by the fact that he had been passed over by the prophet Samuel and that David had been anointed as future king.

*His harp-playing days in the pastures of his father had given him an intimate knowledge of the God whom the giant dared to defy.*

Or perhaps Eliab was thinking of the day that he and his siblings had watched David ride off to the palace with his harp tucked under his arm. Of late it seemed that David spent less time with the sheep and more and more time at the palace.

Eliab must have known that wherever David went, it was always at someone else's bidding. He chose to ignore that fact. He chose, instead, to rebuke this young brother who seemed to be getting more than his fair share of attention.

Ignoring Eliab's remarks, David turned to others with his questions. Very soon someone repeated David's remarks to the king, and Saul sent for the young boy.

By the time he reached Saul's tent, David had assessed the situation from faith's perspective. "Don't lose heart on account of this Philistine," he told the king. "Your servant will go and fight him."

Saul discouraged him. "You can't go out against him. You're only a boy. This man has been a fighting man since his youth."

Did no one understand the situation? Could no one see that this uncircumcised Philistine was defying more than the armies of Israel? He was defying God Himself. Did no one understand that God would fight the giant? That God was not intimidated by this heathen soldier who stood half again as tall as the tallest soldier? That any soldier from Saul's army would be but an instrument in the hand of the One who would do the fighting? David emphasized that the same Lord who had delivered him from the paws of wild animals would deliver him from the hand of the Philistine.

"Your servant has been keeping his father's sheep," David explained. "When a lion or a bear came and carried off a sheep, I went after it, struck it, and rescued the sheep from its mouth. When it turned on me I seized it by its hair, struck it, and killed it. Your servant has killed both the lion and the bear. This uncircumcised Philistine will be like one of them because he has defied the army of the living God."

It must have been a hard choice for Saul. For forty days he had listened while Goliath screamed obscenities across the valley. For forty days he had watched terror multiply in the ranks. Not one of his men was willing to face the giant. Standing before him was the first hope he had seen in forty days. It wasn't much of a hope. Such a young boy he was, and unprepared for battle. No armor. No weapon. Reluctantly, the king agreed. "Go, and the Lord be with you."

The choice was less hard for David. In his father's pastures he had spent many hours contemplating his omnipotent divine Shepherd. He was convinced that no one could successfully defy the God of Israel. It wasn't David's fight. It was God's.

Saul pressed David to be more prepared. He dressed him in his own tunic, put a coat of armor and a bronze helmet on him. David fastened on Saul's sword and stumbled around in his ill-fitting armor.

"I can't do this," David said. "I'm not used to them." He laid the armor aside and went out just as he went to the pastures day by day. He took his staff in hand. In the valley, he paused to choose five smooth stones from the stream and put them in his shepherd's pouch. Then, with sling in hand, he approached the Philistine.

Goliath, his shield bearer in front of him, came closer, looking David over. "Am I a dog?" he shouted, "that you come at me with sticks?" He cursed David and then taunted him. "Come here," he said. "I'll feed you to the birds and the beasts of the field."

David screamed a response born out of his unshakable confidence in God. "You come against me with sword and spear and javelin, but I come against you in the name of the Lord Almighty, the God of the armies of Israel, whom you have defied. Today,

*He was convinced that no one could successfully defy the God of Israel.*

the Lord will hand you over to me, and I'll strike you down and cut off your head. Today I'll give the carcasses of the Philistine army to the birds, and the whole world will know that there is a God in Israel. And the people here will know that it is not by sword or spear that the Lord saves. For the battle is the Lord's, and he will give all of you into our hands."

The Philistine came closer and closer, ready to attack. David ran toward the battle line. He reached into his bag, took out a stone, and hurled it high over his head. With such force behind it, the stone imbedded itself in its mark—the forehead of Goliath. In a flash the giant was down.

David stood over him, drew out Goliath's sword, and severed his head. At once the Philistine army thundered away. With a great shout, the army of Israel surged behind it. David was left to ponder what had happened. In spite of the accusations of his brother, the discouraging words of his king, and the curses of the enemy, he had proceeded in the name of the Lord to do the Lord's business. God had taken care of the rest.

Later, as David stood over the fallen giant, there must have been a certain amount of confusion mixed with euphoria. In the melee that surrounded him as Israel's army pursued the Philistines, David stood alone. In the presence of thousands of soldiers, he

> *David's heart overflowed with the knowledge that God had won the victory.*

must have felt only the presence of God. A part of him knew that the giant had fallen at his hand. Perhaps in the shouts of victory he even heard his name raised. But in that glorious dramatic moment, I believe David's heart overflowed with the knowledge that God had won the victory. God had proved that which David knew in his heart to be true. No enemy is tall enough, strong enough, equipped enough to defy the Living God.

The true climax of this drama is not that moment when a smooth little stone left the shepherd's sling and found its way into the head of the giant. The real climax of this encounter is the speech that David made before he hurled the stone. His words, boldly thrown across the gap, reveal the depth of his trust in the God that the giant defied.

Very often we find ourselves attaching more importance to an artifact than did its original owner. I strongly suspect that this may be true of David's sling. Not that his simple "weapon of war" wasn't important. He did, after all, fell Goliath in a riveting drama in which the sling commanded most of the attention. Still, I doubt that David attached any great importance to the sling. During his harp-playing days in the pastures, he had come to believe that when God chose to do an extraordinary thing, any instrument would do. And when God chose to fell a nine-foot giant, neither David nor his sling had a rightful claim to center stage.

*This story of David's harp is taken from 1 Samuel 16-17.*

# Chapter Eight

# Tokens of Friendship

*I*N A RAGGED SCRAPBOOK FROM MY CHILDHOOD THERE IS A NOTE FROM my first "best friend." Written on a tiny piece of paper and enclosed in a miniature envelope, this note was my friend's parting gift to me. I was ten years old and my family was moving fifteen hundred miles away.

I have had many "best friends" since that day, but Glendora was the first. I treasure this keepsake.

In our collection of old, worn, and tattered books is a small volume called *Friendship's Token and the Lover's Gift*. It was given to my husband's great-aunt Nettie over 120 years ago. As we examined this artifact left behind to be puzzled over by succeeding generations, we concluded that it too was a parting gift from a friend. Nettie was moving half a continent away and her friend Ella inscribed in the book

> Words may pass away
> and every feeling die away
> but the constant love I have for you
> never never shall decay.

I consider the gift of friendship to be one of life's greatest treasures. Of late, my husband and I have experienced a renewed, intense appreciation for our friends. In part, this can be explained by the fact that we have moved to a new community where we have yet to establish a circle of friends. But it also might be explained by the fact that we are at that age where "reconnecting" with old friends becomes a priority. (The urge to reconnect usually surfaces about the same time that the fast food clerks quit asking whether you qualify for the senior discount.)

We have spent the past summer celebrating the gift of friendship. Through reunions, overnight visits, letters, telephone calls, and lunch meetings we have reconfirmed cherished relationships.

In the process, I have been reminded that friendship comes about in different ways. Some friendships develop over time. Some come suddenly. Some come from unexpected places—as from a teacher who inscribed in my yearbook, "I have called you friend."

Sometimes a friend appears at a certain juncture in your life, and afterward you know that this companion on the road made all the difference for you.

# The Warrior's Belt

JONATHAN WAS A FRIEND TO DAVID. THE SORT OF FRIEND WHO MADE A difference. That's why we would expect to find a warrior belt among those things that David left behind. David would have always treasured that belt because Jonathan gave it to him as a token of friendship.

A warrior's belt was an important part of the soldier's equipment and would not have been surrendered lightly. But Jonathan gave his own belt to David on the day that David killed Goliath.

The victory had just been won. The nine-foot giant had made his final challenge and lost. A tight little group had gathered in the king's tent—General Abner, Jonathan, and David, the hero of the hour. A crimson stain ran down one side of David's garment, for he clutched his bloody trophy, the head of the fallen giant, under his arm. Outside, the roar of the retreating Philistines reverberated across the valley.

High drama for the young shepherd boy. But hardly a celebration for there were few there to celebrate

> *A warrior's belt would not have been surrendered lightly.*

his victory. His brothers weren't there. A short time ago they had been there, accusing him of being a conceited little kid bent on mischief. Afterward—after the Philistine leader who mocked the army of the living God had fallen—they said nothing. No apology. No words of encouragement. No acknowledgment of personal or national victory.

Where were they when the giant fell? Did they stand there, grim-faced and silent, watching David? Did they see the small, solitary figure standing alone until Abner came and fetched David to the king's tent? Or did they hurry away after the Philistine army, feeling grateful for an excuse not to congratulate their pesky younger brother?

Being summoned to the king's tent had to be an honor, but the king's first words must have been deflating to the young hero.

"Whose son are you?" Saul asked.

The king should have recognized him.

David had been in his presence before. He had played soft, soothing music on his harp when the king was troubled in spirit.

Perhaps the king had been so troubled that he did not remember. Or perhaps he simply took no note of the boy. So now, he asks, "Whose son are you?"

"I am the son of your servant, Jesse," David answered.

Yesterday, he had been caring for Jesse's sheep. Now, in a daze, he stood in the king's tent. Vaguely aware that he was at the center of the day's events, he answered Saul's question with a simple sentence.

He didn't remind Saul, "I am Jesse's youngest son—the one who played the harp for you." He didn't tell him, "I am the brother of three of your soldiers." He simply said, "I am the son of your servant, Jesse."

What must have been going through his mind as he stood there in that great moment of triumph for himself and for the nation?

It is clear that David would never have assumed credit for the day's victory, but one has to wonder whether he looked for some affirmation from those who should have celebrated with him. If so, he didn't find it. His brothers ignored him. The king didn't remember him.

But Jonathan, the king's son, felt a connection with the young shepherd boy. He determined at that moment that he would be David's friend. He gave him his robe, tunic, sword, his bow, and even his warrior belt. Valuable gifts in themselves, but more so because they were given as a token of friendship.

Jonathan came into David's life at a time when David needed a friend. His need might not have been obvious to anyone but God because outwardly David had it altogether. He was what we would term a perfect ten.

> He was ruddy.
> He was handsome.
> He was uncommonly strong.
> He wrote poetry.
> He was a talented musician.
> Best of all, he had a real heart for God.
> He was every mother-in-law's dream.

David could have won the employee of the year award by any standard. He faithfully performed his duties. He had a mind for details.

(He found someone to care for the sheep when he was called away.) He could be trusted to perform his duties even if it involved personal risk. (He fought the bear and the lion to prevent harm to the sheep.) There was never any reason to worry when David was in charge.

*David could have won the employee of the year award by any standard.*

David was also the perfect son. He did what he was told to do. He did it well, and he never complained in the process.

He was all this before he became a hero in Israel. Before he slew the giant. On the surface, one would not suspect that David had need of a friend. But God looks beneath the surface.

There, He saw a different picture.

There, He saw a David who was overlooked, hardly noticed, even ignored.

For starters, Samuel was less than enthusiastic about anointing one of Jesse's sons to be future king of Israel. It was nothing against David, it was just that Samuel would have preferred that Saul straighten out his life and continue to be king.

Then there was David's father. He gave no thought to his youngest son on the day Samuel came seeking the future king of Israel. "Aren't there any more?" Samuel asked when God did not single out any of Jesse's sons.

"Only the youngest," Jesse replied, "but he's out tending the sheep." Only the youngest. Apparently it never occurred to Jesse that David could be God's choice among all the sons.

Up close and personal, no one gave much thought to David. No one except Jonathan, the king's son.

Jonathan saw something in David that no one else saw. He recognized something of value in David. Others looked at David (and sang his praises) as someone who had won his fifteen minutes of fame by landing a lucky shot to the head of the giant. Jonathan saw David as someone who had taken his own life in his hands, someone who risked that life to fight the Philistine.

Saul was glad for the victory, of course, but he had a short memory. Jonathan, on the other hand, never forgot. On several occasions he reminded Saul how David had risked his life when he confronted Goliath.

Jonathan rejoiced at David's successes. This could not have been easy because not only was Jonathan the king's son, but he was also part of the king's military. Unlike David, Jonathan had trained as a soldier. It was his life. He was good. But David was better. No matter. Jonathan rejoiced

> *Jonathan's joy at David's success was an extraordinary gift that characterized an extraordinary friendship.*

over David's success. Jonathan's joy at David's success was an extraordinary gift that characterized an extraordinary friendship.

Jonathan committed himself to friendship with David. He gave his belt to David as a sign of that commitment. Some friendships are destined to die for lack of commitment. Time and distance erode the relationship. But it was not so with Jonathan and David. It does not appear that they spent much time together, but Jonathan's commitment overcame the obstacle of separation.

Commitment also enabled the two friends to cross class and economic status lines—the king's son and a shepherd boy.

It enabled them to overcome the obstacle of career competition and outside interference. Jonathan was undoubtedly warned repeatedly, "If you want to make it to the top, forget about this man. You'll never be king so long as David is alive."

Jonathan must have been a deeply spiritual man. He understood and accepted what his father could never accept—God had ordained that David be king. Fortunately for David, God had also ordained that Jonathan be David's best friend. Jonathan was willing to take second place to his friend.

Saul's hatred plunged David into a fugitive existence. Two bittersweet meetings occurred between Jonathan and David during the time David was running from Saul. In the first, when the two friends met secretly, both men wept. David bowed three times before Jonathan, and Jonathan reconfirmed his friendship. The second meeting occurred when Jonathan went to find his friend for the express purpose of "helping him find strength in God."

In part, Jonathan encouraged David by laying out the facts of the situation. He reminded David to stay focused on what they both knew to be true.

"My father will not lay a hand on you. You will be king over Israel, and I will be second to you."

The most cursory examination of David's life after he left his father's pasture reveals how great was his need for a friend. Jonathan's friendship sustained David through many trials. It enriched his life, even saved his life at times.

When Saul and Jonathan were slain in battle, David's worst enemy and his best friend died together. He mourned them both.

Of Jonathan he wrote:

> How the mighty have fallen!
> Jonathan lies slain on your heights.
> I grieve for you, Jonathan my brother;
> you were very dear to me.

David's warrior belt was a constant reminder of Jonathan, not just because the belt was Jonathan's gift to David, but because Jonathan himself was God's gift to David.

It is obvious that Jonathan made a difference in David's life. His example reminds me of dear and faithful friends who in the providence of God have been a part of my life. And I am prompted to give thanks that each one, in some special way, has made a difference for me.

*This story about the warrior's belt was taken from 1 Samuel 17:55-58; 18—20; 23:15-18; 31 and 2 Samuel 1:17-27.*

⌒⋈⌒

# Chapter Nine

# The Clock

The Ansonia clock in our living room once belonged to my father's parents. Although few people would notice, the top of the clock's wooden cabinet is not original. The original was damaged by water during a move, and Dad later replaced it with a new, expertly carved piece.

The clock holds a great many memories for Dad. He remembers his parents telling how they purchased this clock when they were first married. They paid $2.50 for it and, at the same time, bought a fancier one for the parlor for which they paid one dollar more.

Dad remembers how his mother kept the Ansonia clock high on a shelf in the kitchen away from the reach of small children. Each night just before she went to bed, she wound the clock.

Always, on Christmas Eve Dad looks at the old clock and recalls the Christmas Eves of his childhood. His parents did all their gift shopping on that day. They hitched up the wagon, rode into town, and were gone until after time for the little ones to be in bed. Dad and his younger siblings were always too excited to fall asleep. The older sister in charge used the "clock formula" to encourage sleep.

"Count the ticks of the clock," she said. And so Dad always fell asleep on Christmas Eve as he counted the ticks of the clock.

The clock still works, thanks to Dad, who has long made it his hobby to repair old clocks. It runs when he is with us as he assumes responsibility to wind it. I must confess that I forget to do so when he is not with us.

When the old clock strikes, it sounds as though it is in a great rush. It always finishes ahead of my battery-operated wall clock. Time in a hurry seems to be the message of my heirloom clock.

I don't want time to hurry. I love this period of my life, and I would like to savor it more.

There are things I want to do. Tasks to accomplish. Books to write. Friends to see. Places to visit.

Every week or so I add to the list. Sometimes, I find myself wishing that I could stop the clock and make time stand still.

But in the history of the world, there has been only one person who managed that. At Joshua's request, God once stopped the great clock in the sky by making the sun stand still.

## Joshua's Javelin

IN BIBLICAL HISTORY, THERE IS A LIST OF STRANGE INSTRUMENTS OF BATTLE: the jawbone of an ass, a shepherd's sling, a tent peg, a broken pitcher that had held a lamp. There is also a javelin that once belonged to Joshua, not a strange instrument but one that was used in an unusual way.

When Joshua was appointed successor to Moses and given the task of possessing the land, he inherited an awesome task. But he was well-equipped for the job because he had faith in an awesome God. From his youth he had assisted Moses, and as a young man he proclaimed an unwavering faith in the power of God over Israel's enemies. As one of twelve spies sent into the land forty years prior, he had urged the people to believe God and to trust Him to overcome the giants in the land. Through forty years of wandering with disobedient Israel, Joshua's faith in Jehovah had grown stronger. Still, a mammoth task loomed before him.

The miraculous defeat of Jericho encouraged the Israelites in the task that lay before them.

Afterward, they came to Ai. The fall of Ai was part of a chain of events that began with Israel's defeat the first time she attacked the city. One man's sin—taking forbidden loot from Jericho—was credited with the initial defeat at Ai.

Defeat might have been avoided had Joshua taken time to ask God for divine direction before going to battle. But there is nothing in the record to show that he did. Some spies who had gone ahead declared, "It's but a

*Through forty years of wandering with disobedient Israel, Joshua's faith in Jehovah had grown stronger.*

small place, you only need to send a few thousand to take it. No need to send all of us." As it turned out, Israel fled before Ai's army that day and three dozen Israelite troops died.

Only then, in the face of defeat, did Joshua inquire of God.

Through God's instructions, Achan's sin was discovered and dealt with. Afterward, God told Joshua how to take Ai.

Joshua's javelin was an essential part of the defeat of Ai. So was the fact that Joshua asked for and followed divine directions.

He took a very large army and divided it to prepare an ambush. The plan called for the main army to march in broad daylight against Ai, draw the army of Ai out, then retreat, pulling Ai's army away from the city. Part of Joshua's army would hide behind the city. Another contingent would hide between the city and the neighboring town of Bethel. Once the army of Ai left the city, the hidden troops would rush the city, capture it, and set it on fire.

Joshua stood in the valley watching the proceedings. When the army of Ai had cleared the city in pursuit of the retreating Israelites, God told Joshua, "Hold out your javelin toward the city." Joshua held it out. Perhaps the sun caught the reflection, signaling the troops. In any case as Joshua held out his javelin, the hidden soldiers of Israel rushed to invade the deserted city.

The soldiers of Ai looked back to see their city in smoke. Then, looking all about, they saw that they were surrounded by Israel's army. There was no hope for escape.

Israel closed in, cut them down, and left neither fugitive nor survivor, save the king whom they brought to Joshua.

Joshua did not draw back his javelin until Israel had destroyed all of Ai. Afterward he hanged the king.

It would seem that the initial defeat at Ai would have made Joshua a bit more careful about seeking God's directions, but the record shows he wasn't quite careful enough. News of the defeat of Ai spread to neighboring people, and a group from a near city, Gibeon, decided to pursue peace with the Israelites rather than attempt to defeat them in the battle that was sure to come.

The Gibeonites had reason to fear Joshua's army. They had heard all about Israel's God. Like the people of Jericho, they were terrified at the thought of pitting themselves against an army that was enabled by such a God. Still, they had reason to believe that a treaty would not be made easily. They resorted to subterfuge.

One day there came to Israel's camp at Gilgal a worn looking group of men riding donkeys loaded with worn-out sacks and old wineskins that were cracked and mended. The riders wore patched sandals and old clothes. The bread in their food supply was dry and moldy.

"We have come from a far distant country to make a treaty with you," they announced.

"How do we know you haven't come from a nearby place? How can we make a treaty with you?"

But the men protested. "Your servants came from a very distant country." They rehearsed all that they had heard about Israel's God. "Our elders and those living in our country ordered us to come and make a treaty with you." As proof that they had come from a great distance, they pointed to their provisions. "This bread was warm when

> *As proof that they had come from a great distance, they pointed to their provisions.*

we packed it the day we left. These wineskins were new. Our clothes and sandals are worn out by the very long journey."

The men of Israel sampled the supplies, but did not inquire of the Lord. So Joshua made the treaty.

Three days later, he learned the truth. The men were neighbors living nearby. When the Israelites discovered this, they were angry with their leaders for making the treaty, but they all knew that by breaking the treaty they would bring down the wrath of God upon themselves so they honored it.

Joshua confronted the Gibeonites, who explained their actions by emphasizing what they had heard: "Your servants were clearly told how the Lord your God had commanded his servant Moses to give you the whole land and to wipe out all its inhabitants from before you. So we feared for our lives and that is why we lied to you. We are now in your hands. Do to us whatever seems good and right."

The Gibeonites were spared, but they were made to be water carriers and woodcutters—slaves—for the Israelites.

When the king at Jerusalem heard about the treaty of peace the Gibeonites had made with Israelites, he appealed to four other kings to join forces with him and fight Gibeon.

He was very alarmed because Gibeon was an important city, like one of the royal cities, larger than Ai, and all its men were well-trained soldiers. With his allies, he attacked Gibeon.

Gibeon, so recently allied with Israel, sent an urgent message to Joshua. "Don't abandon your servants. Come quickly and save us. All the Amorite kings from the hill country have joined forces against us."

God affirmed that Joshua should go. "Don't be afraid of them, not one of them will be able to stand against you," He said.

Joshua took his entire army, including all his best fighters. They marched through the night and took the allied kings by surprise. The Lord threw the men into confusion, and Israel defeated them in a great victory at Gibeon.

Israel pursued the kings and their armies along the road toward Beth Horan and cut them down. Along the way God hurled down great hailstones on them, and more died from the hailstones than from the swords of the Israelites.

*Joshua realized there were not sufficient daylight hours left to accomplish what needed to be done.*

It was all going well. Still, Joshua realized there were not sufficient daylight hours left to accomplish what needed to be done. And he prayed to God in the presence of Israel that the sun and moon would stand still.

God stopped the clock for about a full day until the nation avenged its enemies.

In the record of this miraculous provision, we read, "There has never been a day like it before or since, a day when the LORD listened to a man. Surely the LORD was fighting for Israel."

Thus ends the chain of events that began with the first attempt to conquer Ai.

What began with an error on the part of Joshua, who failed to listen to God, ended with a miracle on the part of God, who deigned to listen to man.

Whenever I think of Joshua's javelin, I am reminded of the day that time stood still. More importantly, I am reminded that very often it takes man longer to listen to God than it takes God to listen to man.

*This story of Joshua's javelin was taken from Joshua 7—10:15.*

# Chapter Ten

ॐ

# Grandfather's Onyx Treasures

*A* SMALL HEIRLOOM LAMP CASTS A SOFT LIGHT ABOUT OUR LIVING ROOM. Although often mistaken for marble, the lamp is made of delicately striped yellow onyx. A matching box sits beside the lamp. Both pieces are items that I remember from my childhood. The box, sometimes called a casket, served as a convenient place to store marbles. The lamp served no useful purpose because some parts essential to its operation were missing.

After the lamp came to me, I determined to add the missing parts. At a little shop in Sausalito, California, my husband and I presented my relic and asked what could be done.

The shopkeeper silently caressed the stone and called his assistant to have a look. Together they conjectured about its origin. "Italian marble?" they asked.

"Onyx," I replied, and told them the story of the lamp. The stone was taken from the Onyx Cave in Crawford County, Missouri, and made into a lamp by my maternal grandfather, who worked in a marble factory in St. Louis. The shopkeepers listened with interest and then, obviously relishing their task, transformed my family keepsake into a working lamp. For the finishing touch, they helped us select a simple shade that would neither overpower the lamp nor detract from its beauty.

The box that matches my lamp has been broken—a fact I regret but for which I must take responsibility. Thinking it the perfect prop for our annual Christmas pageant, I once pressed it into the hands of a youthful wise man so that he might present it to the baby king. Unfortunately, as he practiced his royal entrance, the young actor dropped the box. I found some strong glue with which to repair the crack and vowed never to use it as a prop again.

Today the small onyx casket serves as the perfect container for alabaster eggs from the isle of Capri. To the casual eye, the mended crack goes unnoticed. I, on the other hand, can never look at the box without remembering that it has been broken.

Often, the sight of my onyx casket brings to mind a woman who deliberately broke an alabaster vial and anointed Jesus with its contents. Her story reminds me that spontaneous acts of love create their own soft glow in our lives.

✿

# Mary's Alabaster Jar

SURELY, MARY OF BETHANY HAD CONFLICTING EMOTIONS AS SHE PREPARED for the dinner at Simon's house. It was such a glad occasion whenever they could spend an evening with the Teacher, and tonight He was to be the guest of honor. Still, a pall must have hung over the evening because it was well known that any public appearance by Jesus put Him at risk.

Mary's brother, Lazarus, was to eat at the table with Jesus tonight. That alone characterized the event as a joyful gathering—not only for the fact that Lazarus was again among the living, but also for the fact that his resurrection had prompted many of the Jews to come to faith.

Mary's heart quickened as she thought of her dear brother. How she had wept when he sickened and died—when Jesus did not come in time to heal him. But afterward, when Lazarus was in his tomb and Mary's house was filled with mourners, Jesus did come. As everyone stood weeping and watching, Jesus called Lazarus from his grave. In all the days since, Mary had not looked at Lazarus without remembering the gift of the Teacher.

It had been a costly gift. When word spread about Lazarus' resurrection, the Pharisees determined to kill Jesus. He and His disciples had gone away to a village near the desert, and Mary had not seen Him since that day.

Her heart must have filled to overflowing at the thought of seeing Jesus again. But no amount of joy could obliterate the knowledge that Jesus was putting Himself in grave danger. What could she do, how could she show her love and understanding tonight?

*What could she do, how could she show her love and understanding tonight?*

Something troubled Mary as she prepared for the dinner—something Jesus had said on several occasions. He would suffer many things, be rejected and killed. On the third day He would rise again. Tonight she had a heavy feeling that the time was approaching. One day, perhaps very soon, Jesus would be taken from them.

Suddenly, it came to her. There was one thing she could do for Him. Quickly, she retrieved her greatest treasure from its storage place, concealed it in her shawl and hurried away to Simon's house. Tonight she would have the chance to show her love and, at the same time, show that she understood what Jesus must endure. Perhaps the opportunity would never be given to her again. But tonight it would be hers.

At Simon's house, Mary's sister, Martha, was already busy serving the guests. That was Martha's way. She served. She took care of details. There were always endless tasks that commanded Martha's attention. But under Jesus' gentle teaching, Martha had ceased to complain when Mary paid little mind to those details. Mary expected no rebuke from Martha tonight.

Outside Simon's house a group of Jews gathered. Snatches of conversation revealed that they were vying for the best view—not only of Jesus, but of Lazarus as well. They wanted to see the man whom Jesus had raised from the dead, the man whom the chief priests had determined to put to death along with Jesus.

Inside the house, Mary gazed at Lazarus, reclining at the table with Jesus. Dear Lazarus, whose return from the grave had prompted such a mixture of good and evil. So many had believed in Jesus afterward. So many others had threatened to kill Him.

Clearly this gathering was a bittersweet occasion.

Mary waited for the right moment to perform her lavish act of love. At the proper time she moved to where Jesus reclined. She clung to her most precious treasure—an alabaster jar containing a

*She was to be remembered throughout the world for her lavish show of love.*

pound of ointment, valued at a year's wages. Perhaps her intended action was a bit extravagant, but the treasure belonged to her. She would use it as she pleased. Quickly, she broke the jar and before the unbelieving eyes of the disciples, she poured the contents on Jesus. On His head. On His feet. Then she fell at His feet and wiped them with her hair.

Even as the perfume filled the air, the disciples began to murmur among themselves. Judas was especially incensed. He rebuked Mary sharply for the waste. "It would have been better to sell the perfume and give the money to the poor," he told her. Mary, who had always given more attention to devotion than to detail, was accustomed to criticism but his rebuke stung. Was not this gift hers to give?

The Teacher came to her defense, immediately rebuking Judas. "Let her alone," He said. "She has done a beautiful thing to me. She has done this to prepare for my burial. She did what she could."

It would have been enough that He understood. He would not have had to pay honor to her before the entire company. But He did. "Wherever the gospel is preached in the whole world, what this woman has done will also be told, in memory of her."

I wonder how those words made Mary feel. Once she had been criticized for worshiping when there were tables to wait. Tonight she had been criticized for waste. But now, according to Jesus, she was to be remembered throughout the world for her lavish show of love.

I wonder if tears came to her eyes.

I am not at all certain that we focus enough on Mary as she is seen at Simon's home. Whenever her name is mentioned, we tend to think of that other dinner when Mary worshiped while Martha waited on tables. Centuries after they lived, the sisters from Bethany still give rise to discussion on the relative merits of devotion over detail. As we continue to examine the Mary/Martha dilemma, we invariably conclude that there is need for both personalities. While this is an important truth, I fear that we miss other truths by failing to focus on the Mary we see at Simon's house.

There were four statements made about Mary that night that bear examination. Each in some way gives us insight into her character.

Judas said, "**It would have been better to sell the perfume and give the money to the poor.**" Although Judas is clearly rebuking Mary, we are told that he was not prompted by real concern for the poor. He carried the purse holding the disciples' common funds and habitually helped himself to it. Money given for the poor would surely have found its way into that purse. His rebuke stemmed from greed.

I think that guilt also played a part. Judas looked on as Mary offered her most precious treasure to Jesus and understood that such a lavish demonstration could only stem from a deep love. Seeing love in action reminded him of his own lack of love for Jesus, and he responded by criticizing Mary.

Jesus praised Mary for the beauty of her expression: **"She has done a beautiful thing to me."**

William Barclay describes Mary's action as one of the last acts of kindness done to Jesus. Barclay points out that Mary saw the chance to do something and knew that the chance would come only once. He sees her act as an example for all of us. "It is one of the tragedies of life," he writes, "that often we are moved to do something fine and we do not do it." Specifically, Barclay cites simple things like the impulse to write a letter to thank someone for something that person has done, or to tell someone that we love him or her, or to give some special gift. "The tragedy," he says, "is that the impulse is so often strangled at birth."[1]

Jesus also said of Mary, **"She has done this to prepare for my burial."** The Scofield Reference Bible includes a note on Mary of Bethany, declaring that she alone of the Lord's disciples comprehended His thrice-repeated announcement of His coming death and resurrection. The note points out that Mary of Bethany was not among the women who went to the sepulcher with intent to embalm the body of Jesus. The inference is that Mary understood He would rise again. She knew it was pointless to look for Him in the tomb.

No incontrovertible evidence exists as to how much Mary understood, but it seems clear that she understood more than the disciples. Perhaps her heart was more open because she was not concerned about earthly kingdoms. She had no agenda for the Messiah, this One sent from God. When she sat at the feet of the Teacher, she had only one purpose—to understand and to remember what He had to say.

Finally, Jesus said of Mary, "**She did what she could.**" As a woman, Mary had little opportunity to express what she learned or to act upon that knowledge. But at Simon's dinner, she seized her chance. That night, according to Jesus' own testimony, Mary did what she could.

G. Campbell Morgan honors Mary with these words, "I would rather be in succession to Mary of Bethany than to the whole crowd of the apostles."[2]

I can't help but wonder what happened to that broken alabaster jar. Did anything remain of it when Mary died? According to customs of the day, when a body was anointed for burial, the broken ointment jar was placed in the tomb alongside the body. There it continued to give off fragrance. But in this case we may assume that the broken jar never reached the tomb.

Possibly, Mary kept the fragrant fragments as a remembrance of the bittersweet evening at Simon's house. Possibly, after she was gone, mourners found some alabaster shards with the faint odor of spikenard. If so, they would have been reminded of one woman's spontaneous, lavish act of love.

*This story of Mary's alabaster jar was taken from John 11:38—12:11 and Mark 14.*

# Chapter Eleven

# A Hundred or More Cloth Napkins

$S$ome of our family heirlooms remind me that hospitality was defined very differently in the age of our ancestors. A collection of old cookbooks, including a one-hundred-year-old handwritten "receipt" book, offers clues about the way our ancestors entertained. Dinner menus featured from seven to ten courses. Hostesses prepared elaborate dishes although they had neither regulated stoves nor standardized measurements.

The family china and silverware tell me that to the original owners, hospitality meant Haviland china, pearl-handled fruit knives, sterling silver flatware, and fine table linens.

Over the years we have inherited an enormous supply of old linens:

> a hundred or more cloth napkins,
> dozens of doilies,
> numerous guest towels,
> several damask tablecloths large enough for a dozen place
> settings.

Damask napkins have been perfectly embroidered with the family initial. Cutout embroidery work is found in the linen napkins. Fine cotton napkins are finished with hand-worked scalloped edges.

Fanciest of all are the plate doilies. Before the age of paper doilies, homemakers used a thin fine cotton for making such doilies. Those in my collection feature exquisite samples of drawnwork.

It is because such work is a lost art that I decided to display a small portion of the collection in our dining room. Rather than frame them, I installed several spring rods in the open front of the Hoosier cabinet and hung the samples there. The display provides a constant reminder of the way hospitality was defined in other generations.

I'm glad that the act of hospitality does not depend upon the trappings of our ancestors. Hospitality can be

> *Hospitality isn't about china or sterling silver. It's about sharing what you have with those you care about or with someone in need.*

lavish or it can be simple. I have prepared a candlelit dinner for my five-year-old granddaughter who wanted to get dressed up and eat from a gold-rimmed plate and drink from a long-stem goblet. I have also served my closest friends a meal of soup and bread, using dishwasher-proof settings because it allowed more time to enjoy their company. Hospitality isn't about china or sterling silver. It's about sharing what you have with those you care about or with someone in need.

In the Old Testament, we read about two women who practiced hospitality—a poor widow, and the wife of a wealthy man. They were from dissimilar backgrounds, and the extent of their hospitality was markedly different. But each gave of what she had to someone who had a need. And, in each case, the act of hospitality followed the hostess through some unexpected twists and turns in her life.

# The Treasures of Two Hospitable Women

IF GOD HAD AN ATTIC, I WOULD EXPECT TO FIND SOME FURNITURE AND household artifacts dating from the period of the kings.

Somewhere amidst the kitchen items I would find a common-looking jar used for storing flour and a jug that smelled faintly of olive oil. Both are identified as having once belonged to the poor Gentile widow from Zarapheth who fed the Prophet Elijah.

In the collection of dusty furniture, I would also search until I found the bed, chair, table, and lamp that belonged to the wealthy woman who built and furnished a special room for Elijah's successor, Elisha.

The two women present an interesting study both by their differences and by the things they had in common.

One was rich; one was poor.

One gave out of her abundance; one gave out of her want.

One was a widow with a child; one was married with no child. (As a reward for her kindness to Elisha, God later gave her a child.)

One was a Gentile—a Syro-Phoenician; one was a Jewess.

One was a reluctant hostess; one voluntarily provided a room for the prophet.

> *One gave out of her abundance; one gave out of her want.*

The two women's common experiences were less numerous, but they were more important.

Both women believed in the God of Israel.

Both women had sons who were miraculously restored to life.

Both women showed hospitality to the prophets of God.

Near the village of Zarephath, a poor Gentile widow hurried along in search of sticks. She intended to build one last fire, bake one last cake, and then wait for starvation to claim her life and that of her son. The drought that had dried up the brooks and consumed the crops was about to claim two more victims.

Like many of her fellow townspeople, the widow was caught in a great contest between the worshipers of Baal and the prophet of Israel's God—the God in whom this Gentile widow believed.

Many blamed God's prophet, Elijah, for the drought. He had gone tearing into the palace one day and announced to King Ahab that God would withhold rain because of the Baal worship in the land.

Surely, wicked King Ahab was the real culprit. He, not Elijah, bore the blame for the drought. To begin with, he married a woman even more wicked than himself. She was the daughter of a Baal priest. Furthermore, Ahab built a temple to Baal to facilitate the worship of his wife's god.

> *The drought that had dried up the brooks and consumed the crops was about to claim two more victims.*

Baal's followers believed that their god was the god of rain. So where was he now? There had been no rain since the day Elijah marched into Ahab's presence and announced that a great drought would come over the land.

For that matter, where was Elijah? He had gone into hiding after his impromptu audience with the king. Rumor had it that Ahab wanted to kill the prophet . . . as if that would somehow end the drought.

The widow of Zarephath felt confident that in the end the God of Israel would triumph. But it would be too late for her and her son.

Near the town gates where she gathered her sticks, a man called to her. "Would you bring me a little water in a jar so that I might have a drink?"

As she went to fetch the water, he called again, "And please bring me a piece of bread."

She stopped in her tracks. Perhaps she recognized him as the prophet Elijah. Certainly she recognized that he was Jewish. "As surely as the LORD your God lives," she said, "I don't have any bread. I have only a handful of flour and a little oil. I am even now gathering a few sticks to take home and make a fire, and then I will make the last meal for my son and myself. After that we will die."

"Don't be afraid," he responded. "Go home and do as you have said, but first make a small cake of bread for me from what you have and bring it to me. Then make something for you and your son. For the LORD God of Israel says, 'The jar of flour will not be used up, and the jug of oil will not run dry until the day the LORD gives rain on the land.'"

She went away and did what Elijah told her. She became his hostess for the duration of his time in Zarephath. And all three—the prophet, the widow, and her son—had food enough.

But a great tragedy struck the widow's home one day. Her son died. The prophet to whom she had shown such hospitality went before God and pleaded for the woman. God miraculously brought the son back to life.

This is the first recorded incident of God raising someone from the dead. There would be others, both in Old Testament and New Testament times, but so far as the record tells us, the first was the son of a poor Gentile widow who shared what she had with God's prophet Elijah.

❧

The prophet Elisha enjoyed the hospitality of a woman quite different from the poor Gentile woman who cared for his predecessor, Elijah.

Elisha found himself in Shunem one day where a wealthy lady invited him for a meal. The Shunammite woman, an outgoing gregarious sort, joyfully extended hospitality to the prophet. After that when his travels took him through Shunem, Elisha always enjoyed a meal with the woman and her husband.

Confident that they could do more, the woman approached her husband with an idea. "I know this man is a holy man of God. Let's make a small room on the roof where he can stay when he comes to us." Her husband, undoubtedly less outgoing than she but an obliging fellow nevertheless, went along with the idea. Soon the room was built and furnished with a bed, a table, a chair, and a lamp.

On a subsequent visit, Elisha was so impressed by the woman's kindness that he wished to do something for her in return. But when his servant Gehazi inquired what they might do for her, the woman replied, "I am content with my life."

That wasn't quite true.

She wanted a child. To be childless in Israel was to be the object of pity. Every Israelite woman desired children. But she never said anything. Perhaps she remained silent out of respect for her husband, who was old. Or perhaps she remained silent because she assumed there was nothing that could be done. Perhaps she believed it was her lot to be childless.

Gehazi pointed out the obvious to Elisha. "She has no son," he said. "And her husband is old."

Immediately, Elisha called the woman back and said that in about a year she would have a son.

So intense was her desire that her first reaction was disbelief.

"Don't get my hopes up! Don't mislead your servant," she pleaded.

The next year the wealthy, hospitable woman gave birth to a son. He became a great joy to both parents. When he grew a little, he sometimes went to the field to be with his father. One day in the field he was seized with a violent headache. A servant carried him home to his mother, who sat holding him until he died.

In her dazed grief, the Shunammite woman was sure of one thing—her only hope was the prophet, Elisha. She carried the boy to the prophet's room and laid him on the bed. Then she hurried to her husband.

*She wanted a child. To be childless in Israel was to be the object of pity. Every Israelite woman desired children.*

"Send me one of the servants and a donkey so I can go to the man of God quickly and return."

Her husband questioned the need for the prophet. "It's not time for a feast. It's not the Sabbath."

She assured him that she knew what she was doing.

In a great rush she saddled the donkey and told the servant, "Lead on, don't slow down unless I tell you." They hurried to Mount Carmel, where they found the man of God.

Elisha saw her from a distance and sent his servant to inquire what might be the problem.

But the Shunammite woman's mind was made up. She would talk to no one save the man of God. She took hold of his feet, showing her great humility, and desperate need.

"Did I ask you for a son, my lord?" she asked. "Didn't I tell you, 'Don't raise my hopes'?"

Elisha sent his servant Gehazi ahead with the prophet's staff. "Lay it across the boy," he ordered.

But the woman was not satisfied.

"As surely as the Lord lives, and as you live, I will not leave you."

Elisha hurried along with the woman and on the way met the returning servant who reported that the boy had not "awakened."

Alone in the room with the silent form of the boy, Elisha pleaded with God for the boy's life. He lay prostrate on the boy, mouth to mouth, eyes to eyes, hands to hands. He felt warmth return to the boy's body. He rose, paced the room, and prayed more fervently before prostrating himself once more on the boy. At last, the boy sneezed and opened his eyes.

> *The story of the miraculous raising of the Shunamite's son gained her an audience with the king.*

Elisha called his servant. "Go tell the Shunammite," he ordered. The woman came, bowed to the ground in grateful thanksgiving, then took her son and left the room.

Eventually, the story of the miraculous raising of the Shunammite's son gained her an audience with the king. Some time after the boy was raised from the dead, Elisha warned the woman that she should leave because there was to be a seven-year famine in the land.

When the famine was over, she returned to find that her house had been taken over by someone else, and she went to the king to plead her case. The king was a wicked man who had no use for those who believed in God. In all likelihood, he would have cared little about the woman's plight and would have done nothing for her.

But in the providence of God, she came before the king at the exact moment that Gehazi, the servant of Elisha, was entertaining the king with a story about the woman whose son had been brought back from the dead.

As the Shunammite woman entered, Gehazi said, "Why, there she is. That's the woman whose son was brought back to life by Elisha."

The king asked the woman for more details of the story and listened carefully as she rehearsed them. Afterward, he assigned an official to her case and ordered him to give back everything that belonged to her.

Perhaps that meant the furniture as well. Perhaps that meant that in the little chamber upstairs there was a chair, a bed, a table, and a lamp.

The story that began with an act of hospitality ended with an opportunity to tell a wicked king that there was a God in heaven who had power over life and death.

The widow of Zarapheth and the Shunamite woman offered much-needed hospitality to the servants of God. As a result, each was privileged to witness God's miraculous care in a time of great national and personal tragedy.

One never knows where an act of hospitality will lead, especially if offered in response to God's persistent urging.

*This story about the treasure of two hospitable women was taken from 1 Kings 16:29—17 and 2 Kings 4:8-37; 8:1-6.*

# Chapter Twelve

# Objects of Clay

NOT EVERY ARTIFACT IN OUR COLLECTION COMES FROM A LONG-deceased ancestor. A few items are late arrivals—crudely made clay trinkets, fashioned by tiny daughters now grown, and by an eight-year-old granddaughter, who is fascinated by the potter's wheel.

The ceramic chess set that sits atop an antique wicker library table was painted and fired by our oldest the year she finished eighth grade. It is her daughter who sat at a potter's wheel in Vermont and, under the instructor's watchful eye, shaped her own creations. One of her molded mud blobs is an irregular circle, with the imprint of two seashells, reminding us that she hails from Hawaii. She wrote the words *grama* and *grampa* deeply into the surface and the finished creation sits proudly in our guest room.

A useful, if oddly shaped, bowl made from a mass of clay by our middle child (then in fourth grade) has found its place in various rooms over time.

Without question, the hardest object to explain is my turkey. I know it's a turkey because the six-year-old daughter who created it told me it was a turkey when she first pressed it into my hands and waited anxiously for my approval. It serves no useful purpose save to remind me of how quickly my children have grown or, alternately, to provide a conversation piece. Still it, like the other items, is an artifact dear to a mother's heart.

However crudely formed, these clay objects remind me that God has long used this common, ordinary property to suit His uncommon purposes. He did, after all, take a bit of dust and make a man.

Elizabeth Goodine's song "Praise You" recalls our dusty heritage as well as our noble purpose. "Lord, you formed me out of clay. And for your glory I was made," Goodine writes. And then, with this simple prayer, she reminds us of the proper response to such knowledge—"Use this vessel as you choose."[1]

⟳

# Two Lumps of Mud

THE BLIND MAN SAT WHERE HE ALWAYS SAT. OUTSIDE THE TEMPLE GROUNDS in a prominent place beside the road. There, he begged for alms. Every day he counted off the steps from his parents' house to this place. Every day he sat, waiting for people to give. Whether out of pity or out of duty under the law, he cared not how the shekels came. Whatever he could gain in a day would ease the burden placed upon his parents by a son blind from birth.

He was, at times, subjected to the speculation of passersby, who acted as though he were deaf as well as blind: "Was this beggar born blind as punishment for his own sin, or was it the sin of his parents that caused his affliction?" It was a stupid question asked by stupid people. If a man is born blind, where was the opportunity to sin before the blindness came?

The question came again on this Sabbath day. But this time it was from the group—that tight little circle of men who walked everywhere with the man called Jesus. The beggar recognized their voices at once.

He knew little about the man they followed except that He had created a stir in Jerusalem with His frequent disregard for the rules of the Pharisees. It was one of the followers, not Jesus, who asked,

"Was it this man who sinned or his parents?"

The beggar pretended that he had not heard. He dared not risk the chance of offending the people before whom he begged. He straightened slightly and raised his head as he felt a sudden shade from the sun. The group had stopped directly in front of him. The man called Jesus answered the question. The beggar caught his breath at the words.

"Neither he nor his parents. God had a plan for this man, to display His works in this man's lifetime."

The beggar was conscious of one person stooping in front of him. He waited. Was that a spitting noise that he heard? Had someone spit in disgust at his alms box? He struggled to hide his revulsion.

> *He opened his eyes and saw what before he had only felt. Water. Sun. People.*

Suddenly he felt something cool on his eyes. Mud. It had to be mud. And the one they called Jesus put it there. The beggar recognized the voice again. "Go," he said. "Go and wash in the Pool of Siloam."

The Pool of Siloam the beggar knew. He rose and slowly walked away, counting off the steps to the pool. He washed the mud from his eyes, and when he could feel not a piece of grit, not a remaining particle of mud, he opened his eyes and saw what before he had only felt. Water. Sun. People.

He didn't go back to his beggar's place. He went directly home. I wonder if he counted the steps. He had no landmarks to mark his path. How could he recognize what he had never seen before? How did he find his way, as he "came home seeing"?

Once home, did he look about for landmarks that he had only "seen" with his fingers before? Did he wait for the people next door to speak before he decided with certainty that they were the same neighbors he had always known?

"Isn't this the man who used to sit and beg?" one asked.

"No, he only looks like him," another said.

But the beggar smiled and insisted, "I am the man."

"How were your eyes opened?" they demanded.

"That man, the one they call Jesus, made some mud and put it on my eyes. He told me to go to Siloam and wash. So I went and washed, and then I could see."

"Where is this man?" they asked.

"I don't know."

Inside, he saw the faces of his parents—faces he had often traced with his fingers. He gazed at them. They gazed at him—him with his seeing eyes.

Their reunion was interrupted when people came and demanded that the beggar go with them. It was *"Who dares to heal on the Sabbath?"* the Sabbath and there were some explanations to be made to the Pharisees.

There was no rejoicing there.

No thanksgiving for a healing.

No celebration over the gift of sight bestowed upon the once-blind beggar.

No glad acknowledgments that something extraordinary had happened to the man who stood before them.

There were only hard questions about someone who had dared to knead clay and perform a healing on the Sabbath.

The beggar answered, unafraid. "He put mud on my eyes, and I washed, and now I see."

"He cannot be from God," said the first Pharisee. "He does not keep the Sabbath."

But others argued, "How can a sinner do such miraculous signs?"

So they argued among themselves. They could not condone the actions of any man who broke the Sabbath. Nor could they agree on His identity. Finally they turned to the beggar.

"What do you say about Him? It was your eyes He opened."

"He is a prophet."

Clearly, the Pharisees sought another explanation. The beggar listened as they argued whether he had, in fact, ever been blind. *Blind yes, but never deaf.*

At last they stopped arguing and sent for the beggar's parents.

"Is this your son? Is this the one you say was born blind? How is it that now he can see?"

The parents, so recently exonerated from accusations of the sin that had caused their son's affliction, had heard how the Pharisees determined to put anyone out of the synagogue who declared that Jesus was the Christ.

"We know he is our son," they said. "We know he was born blind. But how he can see now, or who opened his eyes, we don't know." Fearfully, they suggested, "Ask him. He's of age. He will speak for himself."

At this, the Pharisees summoned the beggar again. "Give glory to God," they demanded. "We know this man is a sinner."

This morning he had been a blind beggar, whose plight was largely ignored in the interest of the greater question: "Whose sin caused this blindness?" Now he was sighted and his happy estate was ignored in the interest of the greater question: "Who dares to heal on the Sabbath?"

Perhaps the beggar puzzled over it. *Who am I to discern these questions?* He would tell what he knew and leave the Pharisees to draw their own conclusions. "I don't know whether He is a sinner or not. But one thing I do know. I was blind. But now I see."

"What did He do to you? How did He open your eyes?"

"I've already told you. Why do you want to hear it again?" Boldly now, the beggar asked, "Do you want to become His disciples, too?"

"You are this fellow's disciple! We are disciples of Moses! We know that God spoke to Moses, but as for this fellow, we don't even know where He comes from."

*Now who is blind? How can they not know where the man comes from?* The beggar stood face-to-face with the Pharisees. "Now isn't that remarkable! You don't know where He comes from, yet He opened my eyes. We know that God does not listen to sinners. He listens to the godly man who does His will. Nobody has ever heard of opening the eyes of a man born blind. If this man were not from God, He could do nothing."

> *Something momentous happened then. The beggar confessed, "Lord, I believe."*

"You were steeped in sin at birth," they shouted. "How dare you lecture us!" And they threw him out.

But Jesus came and found him.

"Do you believe in the Son of Man?" He asked.

"Who is He, sir?" the beggar asked. "Tell me so that I may believe in Him."

"You have now seen Him. In fact, He is the one speaking with you."

Something momentous happened then. The beggar confessed, "Lord, I believe."

Meanwhile the Pharisees were left to wrestle with the uncomfortable truth pointed out by the beggar—never before had anyone opened the eyes of one born blind. Furthermore, the man who had opened the beggar's eyes had publicly claimed that He had come into the world so that the blind would see and the seeing would be blind. What could He mean by that?

A number of Jews were still reckoning with the healing of the blind man when Lazarus of Bethany died. Some came to the tomb and stood nearby with the mourners. When Jesus stood in front of the tomb and wept, the Jews recalled the incident of the blind beggar's healing. They asked, "Could not the man who healed a man blind from birth have prevented Lazarus from dying?"

As they questioned the possibility, Jesus called Lazarus to come forth from the tomb. The resurrection of Lazarus caused many Jews to believe on Jesus. But others hurried away to report the event to the Pharisees.

Neither healing nor resurrection touched the hearts of the Pharisees. They continued to question how one who broke the Sabbath could be from God and stubbornly ignored the greater question: "How could a man heal one born blind, unless He be sent from God?"

As for the once-blind beggar, I doubt that he ever again looked at mud without remembering that he had been touched by God—the very God who took a lump of clay and made a man.

If God had an attic, perhaps we would find a pot of dirt in a corner somewhere with an explanation attached, "This is where it all began."

*This story of two lumps of mud is taken from John 9; 11:37-46.*

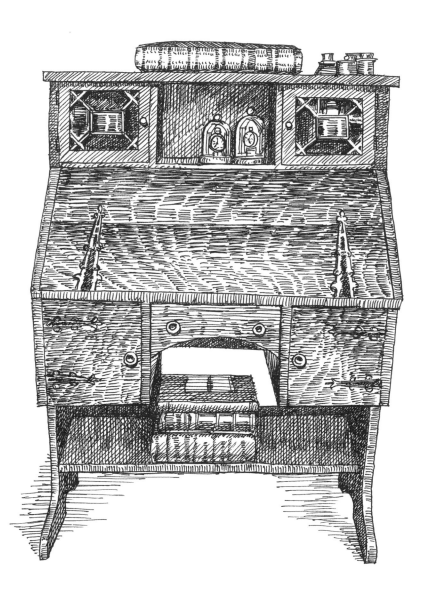

# Chapter Thirteen

# The Attorney's Desk

O UR TIGER OAK DESK HAS THE STRAIGHT LINES, NO NONSENSE LOOK OF mission furniture. But it also boasts leaded glass doors and beautiful fine brass hinges on the drop front. An open shelf above the drop front allows me to display a few old ink bottles and some antique pocket watches. In excellent condition, this desk rates high on our list of favorite heirlooms.

We received the desk from an aunt, but we always think of it in terms of the original owner, a great-uncle who was an attorney in Eureka, California. A silhouette of him, made in Washington, D.C., in 1891, hangs in the dining room. Nearly every room of our house has some item passed down from Great-uncle Frank. But the item we most connect with him is no longer in the family—a letter written by Abraham Lincoln.

As family lore has it, Uncle Frank worked for the War Department while studying law in Washington, D.C. A departmental "house cleaning" took place during that time and obsolete file items were dumped. Among the letters to be discarded was one written by the late President Abraham Lincoln. Uncle Frank, a great admirer of Lincoln, asked if he might have the letter. Permission granted, he encased the letter in linen and carried it on his person for most of his life. The carefully preserved letter was handed down through two more generations and only disposed of in recent years.

The letter was written on December 31, 1863, and addressed to the Honorable Secretary of War. Earlier that month the President had made a declaration granting amnesty to any Confederate citizen who would pledge allegiance to the Union. On the last day of the year, he took pen in hand and wrote a letter of intercession for one such person.

John Tipton, an acquaintance of the President, had lost one brother and seen another crippled for life in the war. Further, his nephew had been conscripted into the rebel service and was now a prisoner of the Union army. Tipton asked that the nephew be discharged from the prison upon taking the oath of allegiance.

After outlining Mr. Tipton's case to the Secretary of War, the President added four words, "Let it be done."

Four little words, spoken on the authority of the President, were sufficient to gain the prisoner's freedom.

A similar letter, divinely inspired, was written by the Apostle Paul. It too is the letter of an intercessor, written with the authority of an apostleship, for the purpose of determining the future of a runaway slave.

## A Letter in Behalf of Onesimus

UNLIKE THE OTHER SUBJECTS OF THIS BOOK, ONESIMUS HAS NO ARTIFACT mentioned in connection with him. As a slave, it is possible that he wore some identifying object such as a slave badge, but the record makes no mention of it. The only thing that is positively tied to Onesimus is a letter to his owner that was written by the Apostle Paul.

Onesimus lived in Colosse. He was one of many slaves owned by a wealthy, Christian man named Philemon. The church at Colosse met in Philemon's home. He and his wife, Apphia, had become followers of Christ under the teaching of the Apostle Paul. In the process, they formed a deep friendship with their spiritual mentor. The couple made no secret of their newly found faith, but nothing they said or did touched the heart of their slave Onesimus.

Onesimus longed for freedom. He dreamed of running away to Rome. He was possessed by his desire to find a new life in the cavernous city. Other slaves managed to lose themselves in Rome and live out their lives without detection. Why couldn't he?

One day the opportunity came. Everything was in place that needed to be in place. If he made his break immediately, he stood a good

> *Onesimus longed for freedom. He dreamed of running away to Rome.*

chance of making it to Rome without fear of apprehension. He helped himself to such provisions as he needed from Philemon's stores. Sure that he had plenty for the journey, he walked away in search of his new life.

He made it all the way to Rome.

For a time he managed to live in obscurity, losing himself in the crowded streets of the city. Everything went as planned until the day he came face-to-face with the man who had brought his master to Christian faith.

We can only conjecture about how Onesimus met Paul the Apostle. Perhaps it was through his fellow townsman, Epaphras. In any event, one day Onesimus, the runaway slave, found himself at the place where Paul, the prisoner, was held.

What Onesimus had avoided in the household of Philemon, he now embraced in the prisoner's quarters. Under the apostle's teaching, Onesimus discovered the greatest freedom of all. The runaway slave came to understand that when Christ Jesus died on a Roman cross, He became the ransom to set men free from sin. With his whole heart, Onesimus came to faith.

An immediate bond formed between the imprisoned apostle and the runaway slave. The bond grew tighter as Paul spent time teaching Onesimus. It grew tighter as Onesimus spent time waiting on Paul, providing much-needed services for the prisoner.

Paul became so attached to the runaway that he began to think of him as his own son. (Paul spoke of only three men as his "sons"— Timothy, Titus, and Onesimus.) He was comforted through the new believer's loving service. He was comforted even more by the thought of having Onesimus with him indefinitely.

But Paul knew the law. By law he was obliged to return the runaway slave to his rightful owner. Paul determined to obey the law. Thus, we have the divinely inspired letter written by Paul to Philemon and to the church that met in Philemon's house.

Onesimus, the runaway slave, returned to Colosse. This time he made the journey in the company of Tychicus, who carried a letter to the church at Colosse. They also took with them the letter written by Paul to Philemon.

It is obvious from Paul's letter that he held Philemon in high esteem and that he found great joy and encouragement in their relationship. Almost a third of the short letter is devoted to a proper greeting for his friend.

Paul's position as the leading apostle would have allowed him to order Philemon to send Onesimus back to Rome where he could be of further service to Paul. He could have uttered those four little words, "Let it be done," but he chose not to do so. Instead, he implored Philemon to welcome the runaway slave, to charge any theft to Paul's account, and to treat Onesimus as a brother in the faith.

In the letter, Paul bluntly reminds Philemon that he owes a great deal to Paul because it was through the apostle that Philemon came to faith. He suggests that perhaps the reason Onesimus was separated from his master for a time was so that he would return as a brother.

While Paul's deepest desire was to have Onesimus returned to him in Rome, he didn't bring up the question of emancipation. He stressed to Philemon that he should welcome Onesimus back as though he were welcoming Paul himself.

Under law Philemon could have inflicted a terrible vengeance on his runaway slave. Some owners whose first inclination might be to treat a runaway slave kindly actually inflicted severe punishment out of duty to make an example of the offender. Clearly, Paul expected more understanding from Philemon. He expressed his confidence that Philemon would do even more than Paul asked in making arrangements for the slave's future.

We don't know what happened to Onesimus. We can only assume, on the basis of the letter to Philemon, that everything turned out very much as the Apostle Paul dictated it. He was, after all, a man with a great deal of authority in the early church.

Of one thing we can be certain—Onesimus found a new life in Rome. The Onesimus who returned to Colosse was a very different man from

> *While Paul's deepest desire was to have Onesimus returned to him in Rome, he didn't bring up the question of emancipation.*

the Onesimus who ran away to Rome. Still a slave, with no right to claim his freedom, he was elevated (spiritually speaking) to an equal position with his master and with the chief of the apostles. As a result, Onesimus gave loving service to Paul, and Paul expected that Onesimus would give the same to his rightful master.

Paul understood about slavery and freedom. He often wrote on the subject. Having lost much of his own freedom by authority of the Roman government, he focused on spiritual freedom and the ransom that was paid for a world enslaved to sin. To the young pastor Timothy, Paul wrote, "There is one God and one mediator between God and men, the man Christ Jesus, who gave himself a ransom for all. ..."

Paul's message of freedom was clear. By Christ's death and resurrection, He became our mediator. For everyone who seeks freedom from sin, Christ declares with unquestioned authority, "Let it be done."

*This story about a letter in behalf of Onesimus is based on the book of Philemon and 1 Timothy 2:5-6.*

# Chapter Fourteen

# The Linsey-woolsey Counterpane

O NE HAS TO WONDER HOW A LINSEY-WOOLSEY COUNTERPANE FROM THE dowry of Ken's great-grandmother has survived 150 years. It came to us over thirty years ago, and I've never quite known what to do with it. Sometimes I display it on top of a trunk or across a bed. But because I am concerned about protecting it, I keep it stored in a cedar-lined trunk most of the time.

An interesting piece of workmanship, it was woven by its original owner. The blue-dyed yarn was made of wool sheared from the family sheep. The graying white linen thread came from flax grown on the family farm. Woven in two panels, the counterpane (or, in current terminology, bedspread) shows slight signs of coming apart at the seam.

It also shows an interesting pattern of wear, suggesting that some tired person frequently napped on top of the spread.

Great-grandmother Mary was a spinster school teacher, living in New York state when, in January of 1850, she received a letter from a recently widowed farmer in Michigan. The story of their courtship has been the basis of many a conversation at Gage family gatherings. But I fear we don't often think about the gravity of Mary's decision when she finally agreed to marry her farmer.

Nearly thirty by the time she married, Mary had had more than enough time to fill a chest with linens. She kept these for that day when she would "go to housekeeping." But there must have been moments when she gave up the idea—assuming that she would spend her life as a "maiden lady." Without a mate, she grew accustomed to running her own life and laying out the course of each day for herself.

Marriage changed all that. With the signing of the certificate, she gained a husband and four children and all the responsibilities that went into keeping a house. The marriage also meant a drastic change of location—from New York to Michigan to California.

Whenever I look at her linsey-woolsey counterpane, I am reminded that in some long ago era, when cross-country visits to family were unheard of, a woman named Mary followed her new husband from one coast to the other. It could not have been easy.

In like manner, a woman named Ruth once made a decision that demanded similar sacrifice. In Ruth's case, she followed her deceased husband's mother to another country, and there found a new husband.

## Ruth's Shawl

PICTURE THE PITIFUL SCENE.

Three women, all widows with no one to care for them. No husbands, no children, no means of support, no proper protection.

They have banded together to travel to a distant country that was once the homeland of the older widow—the foreign one, the Jewish woman.

The older woman is plainly distraught, but there is a bit of hurry in her step as though she is anxious to get on with the journey. One of the younger, Orpah, is pensive, perhaps not yet certain how she feels about the arrangement. But the other walks with determination.

Ruth's mind is made up.

No indecision here.

No second thoughts.

Today she will leave her homeland and go with her mother-in-law, Naomi, to the land of Judah.

For ten years Ruth and Orpah were married to Naomi's sons. Time enough for the three women to bond. Time enough to learn to care for each other. Time enough to become a family.

Their mutual care did not stop when death broke the official tie between mother-in-law and daughters-in-law. As the three women had bonded together in family, so they clung together in the wake of death that robbed them of family.

*The younger women wept at the thought of leaving her. "We will go with you to your people."*

It was not strange that Naomi wanted to leave Moab because it had never been her family's intention to remain so long out of their own country. But circumstances got in the way of their plans as circumstances often do. Now that she had nothing, now that she had no one, now that the news from Judah spoke of blessing on the land and food aplenty, Naomi wanted to go home.

Her daughters-in-law walked with her along the road until Naomi turned to them and bid them return to their homes. She prayed God's blessing on them, acknowledging their kindness both to her and to their now-deceased husbands. "May God give you rest in the home of another husband," she prayed.

It was a gentle "good-bye."

But the younger women wept at the thought of leaving her. "We will go with you to your people," they replied.

"Now, why would you do that?" Naomi asked.

She pointed out the obvious. "Am I going to have any more sons who could be husbands to you? I'm too old to have another husband. And even if I had hope, even if I married tonight and gave birth to more sons, would you wait for them to grow up?"

Once again she urged them to leave, and once more the younger women wept. Then Orpah kissed Naomi good-bye, but Ruth clung to her.

In spite of Naomi's urging, Ruth refused to turn back. Their bond was too strong to be broken. Perhaps Ruth had never before openly expressed what was in her heart. Perhaps she had never told Naomi how much she wanted to be with her. But now she seized the opportunity to declare her love for her mother-in-law.

> Please don't ask me to leave you.
> I will go wherever you go and there I will stay.
> Your people will be my people.
> Your God will be my God.
> Wherever you die, there I will die, and I will be buried there.
> May God judge me ever so severely if anything but death ever separates you and me.

In one short, passionate speech Ruth cut her ties to her own homeland.

It meant leaving her beloved sister-in-law behind.

It meant leaving her parents behind.

It meant leaving her customs and her gods behind.

In that same short, passionate speech, Ruth embraced a new life.

She promised to stay with her much-loved mother-in-law.

She declared her intent to identify with her mother-in-law's people.

She made known her decision to embrace her mother-in-law's beliefs, to put her trust in her mother-in-law's God.

With the matter settled and the bond between them forged to a greater strength, the two women continued on their journey.

Picture the noisy scene.

In Bethlehem the barley harvest is just beginning. Two road-weary women arrive at the gate of the city. Onlookers stare at the pair. The younger is obviously a foreigner. The older is . . . Could this be Naomi? The crowd is astir with curiosity.

Naomi had left during a time of famine. She had gone out with a husband and two strapping young sons. But now, if indeed this is Naomi, she has returned with no husband and no sons. There is only this young woman, a foreigner.

A crowd of women gather around the arrivals. "Naomi!" they cry in greeting.

"Don't call me Naomi," she answers. "Call me Mara, because the Almighty has made my life very bitter. I went away full, but the Lord has brought me back empty."

So, it was Naomi. Older, tired-looking, saddened. But it was Naomi. She had come back to Bethlehem, and the young foreign woman with her was her Moabitess daughter-in-law, Ruth.

> *Two road-weary women arrive at the gate of the city. Onlookers stare at the pair.*

They told Naomi's story all over Bethlehem. And with each telling, they paid tribute to the foreign daughter-in-law who had come back to Bethlehem with Naomi. Ruth the Moabitess became known among the townspeople as the woman who had left her family, her country, her gods in order to stay by Naomi's side—to live in a country not her own, to be part of a people she had not known, to worship a god she had not previously worshiped.

On the road, Ruth had made a passionate speech. In Bethlehem, she went beyond words. She made it her responsibility to care for the needs of her mother-in-law. "Let me go to the fields and pick up the leftover grain behind anyone in whose eyes I find favor," she said to Naomi.

Naomi gave her blessing and Ruth went to the fields. After securing permission from the foreman, she went to work. She worked steadily all morning, pausing only for one short rest in the shelter.

> *Ruth made it her responsibility to care for the needs of her mother-in-law.*

Before noon the owner of the field came around and greeted his harvesters. They returned his greeting, but Boaz was distracted by the sight of a young woman gleaning in his field.

"Whose young woman is that?" he asked of the foreman.

"She is the Moabitess who came back from Moab with Naomi."

Boaz had heard all about the Moabitess and her kindness to Naomi, whose husband was a kinsman to Boaz. He went to Ruth and commanded her to stay in his fields for the remainder of the harvest.

Ruth bowed low to the ground and asked, "Why have I found such favor in your eyes that you notice me—a foreigner?"

Boaz replied that he had heard of all she had done for Naomi. "May you be richly rewarded by the Lord, the God of Israel, under whose wings you have come to take refuge," he said.

In fact, the God of Israel had already begun to reward Ruth. In the providence of God, Ruth had chosen to glean in a field where she would find more than immediate provision of food. She found protection from harm—always a possible threat for the gleaners. A foreigner, she found sympathy from Boaz, whose mother had been a Gentile foreigner. And, unknowingly, Ruth also found potential provision for the future due to the fact that Boaz was a near kinsman.

At the end of the day, Ruth returned home with more than a half bushel of grain. She could hardly contain her excitement as she rehearsed the day's events to Naomi. Upon hearing that Ruth had gleaned in the field of a near kinsman, Naomi must have begun to hope that the future was now secure. She urged Ruth to stay in the field of Boaz where she would be safe.

Through the barley and the wheat harvest, while Ruth gleaned, Naomi thought long and hard about how she could provide for Ruth and for herself. True, Naomi could not give another son to Ruth, but there was a man who might legally assume the responsibility of the two widows. One day she approached Ruth with her plan.

"Go to the threshing floor tonight," Naomi told her. She gave her specific instructions about what to do and what not to do. Bowing to her mother-in-law's wishes, Ruth went and in the custom of the day she let her wish be made known to Boaz. In a word, she proposed to him. And he readily accepted. But there was a proviso. Someone else was first in line to assume responsibility for the widows.

Early the next morning, when she left the threshing floor, Boaz gave Ruth a gift. "Bring your shawl," he said. Then he filled it with six measures of barley and told her, "Don't go back to your mother-in-law empty-handed." When she left the floor, Ruth knew that she would never again be empty-handed.

Of course they were married, and in time Ruth gave birth to a son whom the couple named Obed.

Picture the happy scene.

Once more the women of the town gather around Naomi. Naomi holds her grandson on her lap, and all the women exclaim, "Naomi has a son!" They praise God who has provided for Naomi. "This day He has not left you without a kinsman-redeemer," they said. "May the child become famous throughout Israel! He will renew your life and sustain you in your old age. For your daughter-in-law, who loves you and who is better to you than seven sons, has given him birth."

If Ruth left something behind, I think it would have been her shawl. I think that in dreamy moments she might have rubbed it against her cheek and remembered all the words that Boaz spoke to her from her first day in the field until that night on the threshing floor.

On that first day, the day they met, he said, "I've been told all about what you have done for your mother-in-law." At the threshing floor, the day Ruth proposed to Boaz, he said to her, "This is a great kindness. You have not run after younger men. I will do for you all that you ask. All my fellow townsmen know that you are a woman of noble character." Each time he spoke to her he conveyed his respect and the fact that he saw something of great value in Ruth.

I think that she always remembered the moment when Boaz filled her shawl with grain and promised to provide for her future. Surely, she was greatly comforted by his provision and by his words, "May you be richly rewarded by the Lord, the God of Israel, under whose wings you have come to take refuge."

*This story of Ruth's shawl is taken from the Book of Ruth.*

# Chapter Fifteen

## The Teapot

*M*Y LITTLE BROWN TEAPOT IS ONE OF MY EARLIEST ACQUISITIONS, BUT I can't remember that I ever brewed tea in it. We acquired the pot from Ken's mother during the first summer we were married. We made a quick trip to his boyhood home in Sacramento, and she pressed upon us a few items that she no longer used. Before I had a chance to use the teapot, it was filled with gasoline several times, and I'm not sure that I managed to clean it thoroughly afterward.

On our way back to our Los Angeles home, we intended to visit a logging camp eighty-four miles up the Kern River Canyon above Bakersfield. Our purpose in visiting the camp was to determine God's will for our future.

Actually we had spent numerous weekends that first summer trying to discern what God had for us. Our long-range goal was to go to Japan as missionaries. Our short-range goal was to find some type of related work to gain practical experience. We had checked out several churches that were looking for assistants, including two Japanese churches. Nothing opened up.

One day in a conversation with a professor at Biola (from where we had both recently graduated) a half-hearted question was put to us: "You wouldn't be interested in a logging camp would you?"

"Oh, but we would!"

A Sunday School Union man in Bakersfield was in charge of finding someone for the camp, and he arranged for Ken to preach at the church that met in the school building. The date coincided with our return trip from Sacramento.

Because of a recent earthquake, we took an alternate route that featured a twenty-mile stretch of unpaved road. We came to that stretch just an hour before we were due in camp, ample time to cover twenty miles. Or so we thought. We planned to arrive at the camp in time to visit the Sunday School. As it turned out, we didn't reach our destination until midafternoon.

The road was both steep and full of curves. It seemed at times that the dust through which we drove was as deep as the hubcaps. Our ancient car did not take the challenge so well. It stopped dead in the middle of the road. Ken wasn't long in finding the problem. In order to start the car, he had to prime the carburetor, which in turn required siphoning gasoline from the tank. The exercise had to be repeated every few miles. The only thing we had that would serve as a container for the gasoline was our recently acquired little brown teapot.

By the time we arrived in camp, there was nothing to do but make explanations. We visited the contact from the group of believers and offered our apologies. We also visited the manager of the camp, who would determine whether or not Ken would be given needed employment in order to serve the church.

Later, in Bakersfield, we reported to the Sunday School Union official and assured him that we would be willing to go to the camp church, but they would have to take us sight unseen because we had no intention of making the trip again unless we were moving.

On Labor Day weekend, with the help of dear friends, we moved to our mountain home where we spent the first two years of our married life. They were challenging years in every way, but I was content to stay there forever, had God willed it.

Recently, we made a trip to our former log camp home. I was

overwhelmed by the thought that the camp is both at the top of the world and at the end of the world. I don't relish the idea of making the trip again. But on top of my Hoosier cabinet there is a little brown teapot that reminds me of the reason why we were so content to be there at one time. We had sought the will of God, and we believed with all our hearts that we had found it.

# Gideon's Fleece

WHEN GIDEON'S CHILDREN SEARCHED THROUGH WHAT REMAINED AFTER HE died at a good old age, I wonder if they found a bedraggled fleece of wool stored away in a far corner of his house. His name is synonymous with that scrap of wool. Gideon's fleece has become part of "christianese" as believers intent on discovering the will of God speak of "throwing out a fleece." Like Gideon, contemporary believers often seek some sign from God in order to be sure of His calling on their lives. At times, we, like Gideon, make it harder than necessary to discover His will for us.

Amidst trying circumstances, the angel of the Lord spoke clearly to Gideon—not in riddles hard to be interpreted, but by a plain-spoken message. "The Lord is with you, mighty warrior," the angel said.

Gideon looked all around him, assessed the message in light of the situation, and questioned the messenger. "But sir, if the Lord is with us, why is all this happening to us? Where are all His wonders that our fathers told us about? He brought us out of Egypt, but now He has abandoned us to the Midianites."

From the looks of things it would appear that God had indeed abandoned His people. So oppressive were the Midianites with their allied nations from the east that the Israelites had fled to the hills. They lived in caves if they were fortunate and in mere crags in the rocks if they could not find a cave.

At the risk of their lives, the Israelites came down from their caves and planted their crops. But when harvest time came, the Midianites invaded the country.

They camped out on the land and ruined the crops from Ophrah to Gaza.

They came with their livestock and their tents.

They came like a swarm of locusts. It was impossible to count the men and their camels.

They spared nothing living for Israel—not sheep or cattle or donkeys.

They ravaged the land and so impoverished Israel that the people began to cry out to the Lord for help.

Before God sent help, He sent a message. Through a prophet He reminded the Israelites how He had brought them out of Egypt, driven out the enemies before them, and given the land to them. He reminded them that

> *Now, in answer to their cry for help, God sought a man to do His work.*

He had cautioned them not to worship the gods of the land, but they had not listened to Him.

Now, in answer to their cry for help, God sought a man to do His work. There wasn't much to choose from. There were the Baal worshipers. There were others who didn't worship Baal but who turned their eyes away from those who did. That left only the ones who knew the right and wrong of the situation but were so terrified that they were powerless to change it. Gideon fit best into the last category.

He was secretly threshing wheat in a winepress on the day that the angel of the Lord appeared to him. The first words out of the angel's mouth brought a protest from Gideon. How could God be with him when everything around him cried of God's abandonment? The angel's next words were so clear that he should not have needed any further assurance. "Go in your own strength and save Israel out of Midian's hand. Am I not sending you?"

But Gideon was not convinced. "I'm the least in my family, and our clan is the weakest in all Manasseh. How can I save Israel?"

"I will be with you, and you are going to strike down all the Midianites together."

Still Gideon hesitated. He devised a drawn-out exercise to determine the will of God. First he asked for a sign that it was really God speaking to him. "I'll go and prepare an offering and set it before you. Give me a sign. Don't go away until I come back."

"I'll be waiting," the angel answered.

Not only was the angel waiting when Gideon returned with his offering, but he gave a rather spectacular pyrotechnic show of his divine authority.

"Put the meat and the unleavened bread on this rock," the angel ordered. "Pour the broth out." When Gideon did so, the angel touched the meat and the bread with the tip of the staff he carried. Fire leapt from the rock, consuming the offering as the angel of the Lord disappeared.

Convinced of the identity of his visitor, Gideon cried out in fear. "Ah, sovereign Lord! I have seen the angel of the Lord face-to-face."

"Don't be afraid," the Lord said to him. "You are not going to die."

Gideon responded to this revelation by building an altar that he called "The Lord is Peace." He must have felt hope awakening at that moment. Certainly all of Israel lacked peace at the hands of the invading armies.

The next order struck fear into Gideon's heart. He did as he was told, but he did it under the cover of darkness.

He tore down his own father's altar to Baal.

He cut down the Asherah pole beside it.

He built a proper altar to the Lord and made a fire of the Asherah pole.

Finally, he sacrificed a bull from his father's herd to the Lord.

It was a long night.

An even longer day followed. When the men of the town discovered what had happened, they immediately set out to determine who was responsible. Learning that it was Gideon, they demanded that Joash put his own son to death for demolishing Baal's altar. In a moment of unusual insight, Gideon's father answered, "Let Baal plead his own cause. Let him save himself. If he really is a god, he can defend himself when someone breaks down his altar. Whoever fights for him will be put to death by morning."

By the end of the day, Gideon had a new name, Jerub-Baal, as the men of the town said, "Let Baal contend with him, because he broke down Baal's altar."

Things got worse. The Midianites and all their allies crossed over the Jordan and camped in the Valley of Jezreel.

At this point, the Spirit of the Lord came upon Gideon, and he blew a trumpet summoning his clansmen. In addition, he sent messengers throughout four tribes, calling them to follow him.

Then he got cold feet.

After all the armies had been summoned, after he had decided to fight against Midian, Gideon had second thoughts. *What if this isn't really God's will for me? What if God isn't in this? What if He hasn't really called me to do this?*

Gideon had a little conversation with God about a piece of wool and through every century afterward people have talked to God about fleeces and direction and "is this really what You want me to do?"

"See this bit of wool fleece," Gideon said. "I'm putting it here on the threshing floor. In the morning if the fleece is filled with dew and all the ground is dry, then I will know that You are going to save Israel by my hand."

The next morning the fleece was wet but it lay on dry ground.

Not quite enough. "Don't be angry with me," Gideon pleaded with God. "I have one more request. How about making the ground wet with dew and making the wool fleece dry?"

God is infinitely more patient with people than they are with Him. The next morning the ground was wet and the fleece was dry.

That settled it. Gideon took his men early that morning and camped at the spring of Harod. To the north

*Gideon had a little conversation with God about a piece of wool.*

lay the camp of Midian. Even with the thirty-two thousand troops that turned out, Gideon faced a formidable task.

It soon became more formidable.

"You have too many men," the Lord said. "I don't want Israel boasting that she routed the Midianites by her own strength. Send away all those who tremble with fear."

Twenty-two thousand left.

Like Gideon with his fleece, God was not finished yet. He had one more request. "Have all your men go down to the water," He instructed. "I'll sift them there. If I say, 'this one goes,' then he goes. If I say, 'this one stays,' he stays."

Like Gideon, God made an arbitrary demand. "Separate those who get down on their knees and drink from those who lap the water with their hands to their mouth." Only three hundred lapped with their hands. God ordered Gideon to send the rest home.

Gideon must have had a vision of a fleece, first wet, then dry, because he didn't protest God's decision to reduce his shrinking army down to a mere three hundred men.

God gave him encouragement that night. He ordered Gideon to go down to the enemy camp after dark and listen to the Midianites.

Along with a servant, Gideon went down to the outposts of the camp. There he saw again how the enemy had settled in the valley like a horde of locusts. A sea of camels ringed the tents. As Gideon and his servant came near, they overheard two Midianites talking about a frightening dream. The first described his dream. "A round loaf of barley bread tumbled into our camp and struck the tent with such force that the tent overturned and collapsed."

> *Gideon didn't protest God's decision to reduce his shrinking army down to a mere three hundred men.*

The second replied with utter confidence that anyone could see the significance here. A small loaf of bread causing a tent to collapse? Was that not like little Israel coming against the numberless troops of Midian and her allies? "This can be nothing other than the sword of Gideon, son of Joash, the Israelite. God has given us and the whole camp into his hands."

When Gideon heard the dream and the interpretation, he worshiped God. He returned to the camp, awakened the men and announced, "The Lord has given the Midianite camp into your hands."

He divided his meager army into even smaller units of one hundred troops each. Every man was given a trumpet and an empty jar with a torch inside. "Watch me closely. Do what I do. When we get to the camp and all the men who are with me blow their trumpets, then everyone blow your trumpet and shout, 'For the Lord and for Gideon.'"

The effect was total confusion in Midian's camp. They turned on one another with their swords, then fled.

Gideon and his three hundred men won a great victory for Israel. The Midianites did not return, and the land enjoyed peace for forty years during Gideon's lifetime. Unfortunately, the wool fleece would not be the only artifact that Gideon left behind. In his hometown of Ophrah, he left an ephod, fashioned of forty-three pounds of gold. It provided a singular reminder of the fact that even people who eagerly seek to discern God's will can easily stray from that which is good and right.

After his great victory over Midian, Gideon collected the gold, fashioned the ephod and hung it in his hometown where the people worshiped it. It became a snare to Gideon and his family. Perhaps it was responsible, in part, for the fact that as soon as Gideon died, the people returned to their Baal worship.

The ephod incident reminds us that God uses common, ordinary people—flawed nature and all. It also reminds us that to discern the will of God for one specific action is not the same as discerning the will of God for your life. For that you need more than a fleece. You need a heart that is committed to obeying His Word at all times.

*This story of Gideon's fleece is taken from Judges 6—8.*

# Chapter Sixteen

ᑎᗢᒣ

# A "Vintage Branson" Basket

ASKETS ARE VERSATILE THINGS. THEY ARE USED FOR BOTH PRACTICAL and decorative purposes. On the farm we used bushel baskets to hold everything from shelled corn to soiled laundry. In our northern California home, I decorated my kitchen walls with a collection of small baskets. They are all gone now, passed on to an aunt who loves baskets. The only one left is my "vintage Branson" basket, which we purchased many years ago.

Before the lights of Nashville gave way to the Branson strip, before country musicians discovered the Ozark town, before it became necessary to import souvenir goods to keep up with six million tourists per year, Branson was a sleepy place where local crafts could be purchased at roadside stands. We would have hardly noticed that we were in Branson that day had we not spied a stand featuring hickory baskets.

We stopped and I examined the collection with undisguised longing. What better reminder of my Ozark roots, I reasoned. There was an urgency about my desire for the souvenir because I sensed that it would be a very long time before I returned to the area. My husband, always anxious to please, emptied his pockets and presented me with my new treasure.

The well-woven basket has survived the years and, as all good hickory baskets do, has darkened with age. Over the course of time, it has held many things. From lilacs to linens. From Christmas cards to pyracantha berries. From root vegetables to rolling pins.

It has served both a useful and a decorative purpose and has been used in various rooms of the house.

Today it sits on our antique wooden icebox in the kitchen. It holds a collection of pasta rollers made by my late brother. Ron was the only one of our family to return to the land of our birth. In his later years he lived in the Branson area and marketed his pasta rollers and other woodenwares at Silver Dollar City. I am reminded daily of him, a sibling with whom I fought too much but who was fiercely protective of me and who influenced my life in small but important ways.

If God had an attic, there would be baskets in it. Perhaps one that had been used in the tabernacle for presenting bread offerings. Or one the diciples used to gather the remaining fragments from a miraculous meal that fed thousands. Or the large one in which Paul was let down over a wall. Or perhaps one that became a floating bassinet and held a tiny baby boy while his sister stood nearby in hopes of somehow protecting her sibling from whatever harm the day might bring.

◦◦◦

# Jochebed's Floating Bassinet

JOCHEBED'S THIRD BABY WAS BORN INTO SUCH PERILOUS TIMES THAT HE surely would have died had he not been both an extraordinary child and one born of extraordinary parents. Jochebed and Amram are singled out in Hebrews 11 as people of great faith because they fearlessly defied the king's orders.

Certainly, as slaves of the great Pharaoh, they had every reason to fear the king. He had long controlled their every working hour. But when he set out to control the size and makeup of their families, Jochebed and her husband made a dangerous choice. They disobeyed the king.

To disobey the king was not something to be considered lightly. On the other hand, when obeying the king meant disobeying God, Jochebed and Amram knew that there was only one choice.

The couple already had a daughter and a three-year-old son when Pharaoh ordered all male slave babies to be killed at birth. It was not a good time for a slave woman to be pregnant. But Jochebed was pregnant again.

What did she think as she gazed into little Aaron's face after the new life within her began to stir? Did she breathe a prayer of thanks that he had been born before this latest edict was handed down by the cruel king?

> *When obeying the king meant disobeying God, Jochebed and Amram knew that there was only one choice.*

Did she hope quite fervently that the child growing within her would be a girl?

Jochebed must have borne the birth pangs with clenched teeth silence, praying all the while that no spying eyes would discover her newborn. Certainly when the child pushed forth from her womb, no one would have uttered the joy cry to greet the infant boy. Surely Jochebed met the moment with raw resignation. She recognized that this extraordinary child would be allowed no more than a brief and precarious interlude with them. She knew it. Amram knew it. There was no escaping it. The only uncertainty lay in the question of when and how the interlude would end.

Jochebed faced the uncertainty with determination. She would bear it. Had not her life, indeed the life of every slave, been spent in surviving one day at a time under the iron hand of the king? She would trust in God. And she would do what she could.

She and Amram had little to offer their infant child save the shelter of their hut, and even that was a sacrifice because there was no place in the slave quarters where a newborn boy might safely cry. Each day she held her baby tightly to her breast, shushing his tiniest whimper for she knew that keeping him safe meant keeping him quiet.

Each night she held him until he slept, then slept herself, knowing that for one more day she had safely silenced his cries.

For one more day she had done all that she could do.

For one more day, it had been enough.

For three months it was so. All the while as Jochebed nursed her infant son, she pondered her next step. What would she do when she could no longer keep him hidden from prying eyes, when she could no longer hold him tightly enough to silence his cries?

> *Each night she held him until he slept, then slept herself, knowing that for one more day she had safely silenced his cries.*

A plan, born of necessity, grew in Jochebed's mind. First a basket, just the right size, deep and sturdy. Then the pitch, meticulously applied to the basket's outside until not a drop of water could penetrate. And above all, the pleading with the God who knew when the day would come, who alone could do what a mother could no longer do.

One morning, with heaviness of heart, Jochebed lay her baby in the carefully prepared basket and went to the river. Quickly, she placed the basket in the water.

The dreaded moment had come.

She could do no more.

She cast her child onto the mercy of a loving God. She dared not linger, lest she arouse suspicion. Her daughter, Miriam, stood at a safe distance to keep watch. Jochebed turned her back and walked away, pleading all the while with the God who knew.

Surely He could protect one little baby.

Surely He would silence the cries of her infant son.

The baby awakened. Perhaps it was time to suckle his mother's breast. Perhaps the stirring of the rushes by the princess and her maidens startled him. Perhaps someone tugged at the basket. Something awakened him and he cried.

The cry that his mother had so long tried to silence floated over the water and publicly announced his presence to the one person in all the country who would openly defy the great ruler's orders.

The princess waited as her maiden fetched the basket, then looked into the face of the tiny slave child and felt his cry pull at her heart. Unconcerned about her father's orders, certain that he would indulge her every wish, she laid claim to the child.

The most pressing matter, the need for a wet nurse, was easily resolved when a young slave girl happened by and offered to find someone to nurse the baby. Soon she returned with the willing nurse, and the princess bade the slave woman take the baby home and nurse him until he was weaned.

Obediently, Jochebed carried the baby away. Back in the slave quarters, she nursed her infant son, pondering what God had done. This child, this extraordinary child, had survived the precarious interlude, and somehow Jochebed knew that his journey with God had just begun. Joyfully now, she cuddled him and, without fear, she listened to him cry.

At the end of his life Moses wrote a psalm in which he acknowledged, "Lord, thou hast been our dwelling place in all generations."

Interesting words coming from a man who had known so many different dwelling places. From the slave hut to the basket to the palace to the tents of Midian and then to crudely fashioned places of refuge in the desert, Moses knew a variety of shelters. At the end of his life he felt it necessary to remind the Israelites that wherever they dwelt, "The eternal God is our refuge. . . ." One has

*Did he remember that his journey with God was made possible by two parents who walked fearlessly with God?*

to wonder whether he remembered his own roots as he spoke those words.

Did he remember the story from his mother about a basket that had been his refuge for a brief and precarious interlude?

Did he remember that his journey with God was made possible by two parents who walked fearlessly with God?

I think that Jochebed always knew that her son was destined to accomplish some high purpose. But she may never have dreamed to what extent God would use Moses. There can be little doubt about which keepsake would have been most special to this woman. In all likelihood the floating bassinet went home with Jochebed when she was engaged by the princess to nurse the Hebrew child.

Through all the years of separation from him, the basket would have reminded Jochebed that God had honored her faith and had protected her baby boy.

To a great extent, Moses' mother serves as an example to mothers everywhere. Our children are with us for such a brief interlude although, thankfully, not so brief as in Jochebed's case. We love them, we try to teach them, and one day we let them go. No matter how much we might want to protect them from their own mistakes or from the waiting world, we can no longer serve that function.

Like Jochebed, we come to that place where we say, "I have done all that I can do. The rest is up to God."

On that day we thrust our child onto the mercy of a loving God.

*This story of Jochebed's floating bassinet is taken from Exodus 2:1-10; Hebrews 11:23; Psalm 90:1 (KJV); Psalm 91:2 (KJV).*

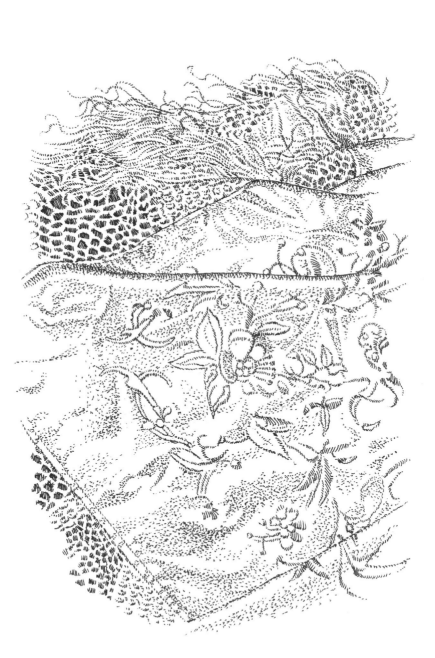

# Chapter Seventeen

# The Shawl and the Cedar Chest

O N TWO SEPARATE OCCASIONS, I PASSED ON A FAMILY HEIRLOOM BECAUSE of a sudden confrontation with mortality. The first time it was my own mortality that was threatened. The second time it was my daughter's.

Fifteen springs ago, the doctors informed me that I had Hodgkin's disease. Somehow, I didn't believe them. I was already past the age when people get that disease. Besides, I was in the middle of a book project. I had a series of retreats booked. My oldest daughter was scheduled to receive her doctor's degree in June. I had no time for dealing with matters of mortality. I went into complete denial.

The doctors tried to get my attention with such words as *lym phoma, cancer, and radiation,* while I moved through each day in a robotic trance. Various specialists took charge of my life, telling me where to go, which doctor to see next, what treatment would be required. I experienced a terrible disconnect from the proceedings. I felt as though I were standing in a corner watching while the ominous events happened to another person.

When I conceded that, indeed, I was facing an uncertain future, I focused on daffodils instead of on the disease. *I may not live to see another spring,* I thought. *And I haven't planted any daffodils for eight years.*

Next, I focused on my daughter. *I may not be around to see her graduate in June.* It was not a very rational thought since the disease doesn't progress that quickly. But it was this second thought that prompted me to give an heirloom silk shawl to our daughter as a graduation gift.

Becki had often asked to borrow the shawl. She would drape it over her shoulders as the final touch of a striking ensemble. I had already decided that someday the shawl would be passed on to her. But had I not been confronted with my mortality, I would have kept it for a number of years. One

> *There is nothing like a brush with mortality to make one see that every day is a gift from God.*

day, all denials put aside, I decided that I wanted to be there when she received it. I wanted to see her face. I wanted to experience the joy of knowing she would wear it and treasure it.

As I write these pages, fifteen years later, it is spring again. There are daffodils blooming in my garden. I am well and Becki, now living in Hawaii, still enjoys her shawl.

Our youngest daughter's bout with breast cancer prompted me to give my cedar chest to our granddaughter. Two years ago Carrie discovered a lump and within a few weeks found her life being run (and fought for) by a team of specialists. Amidst her course of treatment, she was struck by the uncertainty of being around to see her daughter grow up. By the time the treatment was completed, and she had resumed a somewhat normal life, she had a mental list of things she wanted to leave her daughter. Among other things, she wanted a cedar chest in which to put some treasured mementos.

It seemed an appropriate time to pass on the cedar chest that had belonged to my mother. My father had given the chest to Mother on her fortieth birthday. A brass plate attached inside the chest, reads "Frank to Jurine, 6-17-51." My husband did some needed refinishing on the chest and had another plate inscribed with the words,

"Chelsie Jackson, great-granddaughter of Jurine, 5-99."

We presented the chest to Chelsie the week that she graduated from eighth grade. We have requested that she add another plate when she passes it on to a child of her own some day.

There is nothing like a brush with mortality to make one see that every day is a gift from God. Such an experience heightens the simple pleasures that grace our day-to-day existence. To face death is to see life from a new perspective. For those who have put their trust in Jesus Christ for eternal life, a brush with mortality is also a reminder of Paul's words to the Corinthians: ". . . when this mortality shall put on immortality, then shall be brought to pass the saying that is written, 'Death is swallowed up in victory.'"

## Mary's Memories

MAX LUCADO POSED TWENTY-FIVE QUESTIONS TO MARY.

Songwriters Mark Lowry and Buddy Greene ask, "Mary, did you know that your baby boy would one day walk on water?"

I, in turn, would like to ask my own questions of her. These are burning questions that mothers everywhere would ask, such as, "At what point did the joy of a handmaiden turn to the sorrow of a mother?"

When you said, "I am the Lord's servant, may it be to me as you have said," did you have any idea that parental pain would be part of your lot?

When did you first know that your immortal son would die a mortal's death?

When the angel told you, "You are highly favored of God," did you know that your favored status would bring you to a rugged hill where your son would be crucified before your very eyes?

When you were told that the Lord would give Him the throne of His father David and that He would reign over the house of Judah forever, did you think that you would be mother of a God-King who would rule on earth in your lifetime?

When you learned that you, a virgin, and your old and barren cousin Elizabeth were both to give birth—when the angel told you that nothing is impossible with God—did you take that to mean that only good things could happen to these two sons of miraculous birth?

*Did it occur to you that even blessed women experience sorrow if they are mothers?*

When Elizabeth said to you, "Blessed are you among women," did it occur to you that even blessed women experience sorrow if they are mothers?

When she said, "Blessed is she who has believed what the Lord has said to her will be accomplished," did you have any idea what God intended to accomplish?

When you sang, "My Spirit rejoices in God my Savior," did you know that the child you would bear would die in order to become your Savior?

When you sang, "From now on generations will call me blessed for the Mighty One has done great things for me," did you know there would be some "not so great things"?

When you laid your firstborn in the manger, did you know that He would become the "first born from the dead"?

On the eighth day when you named Him Jesus, did you remember that the angel had told Joseph that this child would save His people from their sins? Did you have any idea what that entailed?

When Simeon held your infant son and said, "My eyes have seen your salvation, a light for revelation to Gentiles and for glory to your people, Israel," why did you marvel at his words? What struck you most about his statement?

When he said to you, "And a sword will pierce your own soul too," did a chill clutch your heart?

Was that when you first knew that your son would suffer many things?

Is that when you first knew that your baby son, the Son of God, had come into the world only so that He could die for the world?

Did you think that you had let God down when you lost track of His Son for three days?

Why did you refer to Joseph as "your father" when you spoke to Jesus?

Did you feel rebuked when Jesus asked you, "Don't you know I must be about My Father's business?"

Did you know then that His Father's business would take Him to a wooden cross on Golgotha's hill?

Did you worry about Him when He was forty days out in the desert alone?

Were you frightened when the people from the synagogue in Nazareth drove Him out of town and took Him to the brow of the hill to throw Him over?

When He walked away unharmed, did you assume He was immortal?

Did you assume that no harm could ever come to Him?

When the Pharisees questioned His authority in the temple, did you want to defend your son as the Son of God?

When He raised a widow's son from the dead, did you think He would always exercise power over death?

Did He bring His disciples to your house?

Did you look at one of them with a mother's instinct and know that he was not good company for your son?

Did you feel a wrenching away when Jesus said He had no place to lay His head—when He rebuked a man who wanted to spend time with his family?

When you took your other sons and went to Capernaum to bring Jesus home, did you believe that you could convince Him to get more rest and take care of Himself?

When He refused to come, did you know that your motherly responsibilities had come to an end?

Was it hard to let go even though you knew this was the Son of God?

When He talked about division in families, did you feel you had already experienced it?

When did you first learn of His arrest?

Who went with you to the cross?

Were you comforted by His concern when He charged John with your care?

When He said, "I thirst," did you remember a small boy asking you for a drink?

Did you try to talk to Him on the cross?

Did you cringe when the soldiers pierced His side? Did you whisper a prayer of thanks that they didn't break His legs?

*Was it hard to let go even though you knew this was the Son of God?*

Did you see Him laid in the tomb?

Who walked home with you from Golgotha's hill?

Did you weep through the night?

Did you feel favored and blessed among women that night?

Were you at John's home when Mary Magdalene came running to tell him that the tomb was empty?

Did you know then that the Savior of the world had crossed the chasm between mortality and immortality?

Did you see Him in His resurrection body?

When did you know that death had been swallowed up in victory?

When did the sorrow of a mother turn to the joy of a handmaid?

Did you save some treasured keepsake from His days as a carpenter, or were you content with a mother's memories and a believer's hope?

*This story of Mary's memories is taken from Luke 1:26-56; 2; 4; John 19:28; 20:18; Mark 3:21, 31-34.*

# Notes

## Chapter 2: The Widow's Oil Cruse

[1]Annie Johnson Flint, "He Giveth More Grace," quoted in *But God* by V. Raymond Edman (Grand Rapids: Zondervan, 1962).

## Chapter 3: Paul's Undelivered Letters

[1]Will Durant, *Caesar and Christ* (New York: Simon and Schuster, 1944), 592.

## Chapter 10: Mary's Alabaster Jar

[1]William Barclay, *The Daily Study Bible, The Gospel of Mark* (Edinburgh: The Saint Andrew Press, 1954), 341-342.

[2]G. Campbell Morgan, *The Gospel According to John* (New York: Fleming H. Revell Co.), 208.

## Chapter 12: Objects of Clay

[1]Elizabeth Goodine, "Praise You" (Brentwood, Tenn.: Word Music, New Spring Publishing ASCAP, administered by Brentwood Music, 1992).

## A Personal Note From the Author

### Heart

After college, I spent a year as a children's Bible teacher. During my first week, my partner suggested that *The Child's Story Bible*, by Catherine E. Vos, would be helpful in my lesson preparation. I was fascinated by the details that Vos included, but I was also skeptical. I assumed that she embellished the biblical account. Much to my surprise, when I checked the references I found that Vos had been completely true to the text. That experience revolutionized the way I read my Bible. I began searching out the details as well as the doctrine. This practice has contributed greatly to the fact that the Bible continues to be ever new and exciting to me.

### Soul

Isaiah the prophet wrote, "O Lord, you are our Father. We are the clay, you are the potter; we are all the work of your hand" (Isa. 64:8). It matters not that we each have different strengths and different talents. He shapes us and uses us for His purposes. And that is an uncommon, extraordinary thing!

### Mind

You may have noticed the Bible references for each story at the end of the chapters. I encourage you to read these biblical accounts for additional insights into God's working in His people. If you know the stories well, look for the details as well as the doctrine. You may be surprised at what you see in this new way of reading.

 Strength

I hope that as you have read about the artifacts that were connected to these biblical characters that you have become more aware of one fact: God can take a common, ordinary person who has little or nothing in hand and accomplish His uncommon, extraordinary purpose. If that encourages you in your walk, then the purpose of this book will have been met.

Dear Lord,
As I visualize my readers, I see women who are moms, women who serve in the workplace, and women who do both. I know that every woman contends with her own set of challenges, whether it be time, health, or circumstances. I am so grateful that You are concerned about the details of our lives. I pray for each reader, that Your Word will be ever new and exciting, and that it will be a source of learning, direction, and encouragement. Amen.

*Joy*